This little book by the experience̤.̤ ̤.̤.̤ Dorit Winter, is a very witty little gem.

In literary and imaginative language, Winter leads the reader to an understanding of the difference between training and education. This she does by means of her own experiences with her dog, Scamp. The scenes she describes are so amusing and recognizable, the leap to educating children so well-founded, that one might think this book ought to be required reading for all new parents.

The writing is wonderfully humorous and intelligent and includes insightful commentaries about our times. Among other things, Winter describes the "weather" in the classroom; the deluge of expectations placed upon the child; genuine love vs. infatuation; pampering as a form of neglect; the industrialization of food and pleasure; being cool; and how children survive their childhood.

In short, a wonderful book that I warmly recommend.

Master teacher, author, international lecturer, father of five, grandfather

Train the Dog, but Raise the Child *is a wonderfully direct, humorous and heartfelt reminder of how important common sense is in supporting children as they grow toward a healthy adulthood. Personal insights and practical suggestions gleaned from decades of working with children and parents are interwoven with observations garnered from current public observers of the "state of childhood." No matter the age of your children or grandchildren, or the level of your interest in training a dog, Dorit's book is a "good read" and delightfully jargon-free.*

Mother, grandmother, avid reader

We're told the human being is either an animal or a computer: paradigms that inform much of education today. Dorit Winter examines these tropes in this conversational, enlightening and thought-provoking gem of a book by comparing and contrasting her experiences training her rascally dog Scamp and her years of teaching children and adults. She rightly, I think, calls attention to the incessant attacks on the very qualities that make us human and not animals or CPUs. And she does so in a style that is at once approachable and challenging.

As the father of young boys and a dog owner, I found myself thinking "absolutely!" at parts and "I hadn't thought of that" in others. But the book is for anyone. Teachers, parents, or anybody interested in a refreshing, challenging and frank conversation about what it means to be human.

Father of two young boys, dog owner

Parents, at last! A Manual on simple ideas for raising children! Dorit Winter's new book contains essential guidance for parents, caregivers and teachers. The stories about her dog's antics and her dog-owner learning curve create an entertaining backdrop for readers as they are reminded of key back-to-basics advice on raising children. Dorit penetrates the realm of the growing child with invaluable and concise insights. As a classroom teacher and parent, I found countless examples to help me support the children in my care and lead them in a healthy direction. The children of readers who practice what is conveyed in this book will be healthier and more well-adjusted human beings as a result.

Teacher, mother of two adolescents

Also by Dorit Winter

Because of Yolande
The Art and Science of Teaching Composition
Sheets of White Light
Fire the Imagination, Write On!

Train a Dog,
but Raise the Child

A practical primer

Dorit Winter

dandelion
publications

Train a Dog, but Raise the Child: A practical primer
by Dorit Winter

Contact dandelionpublications.info@gmail.com, www.dandelionpublications.com

Front cover and other touch screen line drawings by Margrit Häberlin
Final illustration by Sean Chiki
Author photos by Afshin Jalalian

..

ISBN-13: 978-1545441992
ISNB-10: 1545441995

Published in the United States of America

For Aleksei and Lucia

Table of Contents

Preface 11

1. Why Not Eat the Chocolate First? 13

2. Training – More Than Potty 19

3. Getting Acquainted 25

4. A Child is Not a Dog 31

5. Pedigree or Pedagogue 39

6. Firmness, Fairness, and Consistency;
   Practice and Repetition 47

7. The Need for Objectivity 57

8. Child Whisperers 65

9. No One Takes Me Seriously 77

10. Tight Ship, Tight Leash 81

11. Treats and Punishments 91

12. Growling, Barking, Baring Teeth 103

13. Be Cool! 115

14. Food 127

15. Anticipation 137

16. Yes, but Do They Love Me? 151

17. Taking the Show on the Road,
    Taking the Road to the Show 159

18. Process 183

19. The Habit of Distraction, the Loss of Mindfulness,
    and the Impact on our Children 189

Acknowledgements 211

About the Author 213

Preface

Although Scamp, my dog, is the lead actor in this book, this is not a book about dogs. Children are the real focus. The book is addressed to their grown-up handlers, the parents and teachers who guide our children out of their blissful state of infant irresponsibility, through the challenges of childhood, and into their own unique, self-determined biographies.

How does a child learn the unnatural requirement of raising a hand to speak in class? How does the dog learn to tolerate a leash?

The dog will never speak in class, and the child should not be leashed.

Nevertheless, training dogs and raising humans have startling areas of congruence. Mothers, fathers, teachers, caregivers, anyone working with children, I thought, might want to partake of lessons Scamp taught me.

This book is my attempt to convey both the lessons and their applications for school, home, and most significantly, for life.

Chapter One
Why Not Eat the Chocolate First?

Children have a mind of their own, without question.
What they lack is judgment. And no wonder. Once you
know what's right, you're stuck in a dilemma. Once you
know there is a right and a wrong, you're not in Eden
anymore. Naïve naughtiness and innocent mischief are no
longer yours to flaunt. Now you have to stop and think, to
ponder, to consider, to agonize. Do I do what's right, or
do I do what I want?

My dog, Scamp, has no qualms about that. He knows what
he wants. He wants to eat. He's voracious. When he eats
what's not part of his authorized diet, the messy results are
my problem. Scamp has an incredibly delicate stomach,
and an incredible lack of good sense about what to eat. He
doesn't discriminate. Rotten crab at the beach is as
attractive as the last M&M lurking in the ivy at the park.
And as every dog owner knows, chocolate is highly toxic
to dogs.

Yesterday I joined my friend Yelena and her two children
for lunch at the nearby Farmers' Market. I observed with
amused awe as two-year-old Lucia determinedly avoided a
healthy snack of sliced peaches to deliver brownie crumbs
from her older brother's plate into her mouth. She wasn't
being sneaky, just intent on the prize. She knew exactly
what she wanted. No dilemma for Lucia. No dilemma for

Scamp. That is their power, they are thoughtlessly decisive, effectively relentless, unabashed in their determination to prevail. They will whine you into submission.

Morality, a free choice for the good, is a major ingredient in maturity. It's the weighty privilege we earned, individually and collectively, when Eve munched that apple. It's a major ingredient, but not a natural ingredient. For both child and pet, doing what's right is an added ingredient. The education of a dog stops at training; the education of a child begins with training and, optimally, eventually, leads to self-reliance, especially in matters of morality. The less self-reliant we are, the more we invest institutions – religious, political, ideological – with the authority to tell us what to do; a dubious trend, a trend with tragic consequences worldwide. "Just say no" is easy enough to say, and wretchedly difficult to bring about. Children, as parents know, fear, and desire, have to outgrow parental authority. And without parental *authority* children are indiscriminately impressionable. Even infants pick up morés from their surroundings. That's why habits of uprightness in the home, before the child is old enough for institutional care, followed by habits instilled in school, are so critical. Habits lay the foundation for tact, empathy, and, ultimately, for compassion and thence morality. That's what education *ought* to be about. What's the use of all the knowledge in the world if it leads to evil? The tree of knowledge, which Wikipedia cannot match for impact, brought us not just an irresistible apple, but also the capacity to distinguish good from evil, right from wrong. The latent capacity for self-determined judgment became our lot.

Scamp is not self-reliant. He has initiative but he lacks judgment. To the extent that he is now pretty well trained, I am his authority. That's as it should be. That's as it will remain. To the extent that Scamp knows what I want him to do, he can distinguish right from wrong. He's not allowed on the couch except when I'm sitting on it. But he's not stupid. If I've forgotten to spread the preventive pillows, he'll take advantage without a second thought. He knows what I want him to do because when he does the right thing he gets a treat. My scolding voice can stop him in his tracks. A mere gesture will prevent him from begging at the table.

When I first got Scamp, he was six months old, abandoned and crazy wild. Now he's four-and-a-half, a "good boy" who knows not to bite the hand that feeds, a dog who respects and dare I say, loves his master, his authority, me. Occasionally he still practices selective deafness, and runs away when I call him. He doesn't know what's right, but he's been trained. His authority is external. Me! I'm his authority! He knows the routines. To be fed, he must stay out of the kitchen until he's called. To leave the house, he must sit until the door has been opened and he's invited to step out. If the door is open and a dog is being walked past the house, though, Scamp will be out in a flash, barking and carrying on. Nor will he hold back from a morsel accidentally dropped on the kitchen floor. He's an opportunist. Conscience is not part of his kind.

His scope is limited. He will never let the cat eat his treat, no matter how hungry she is. In time, Lucia will, most likely, offer her brother a grubby handful of chocolate brownie crumbs. Aleksei, Lucia's brother, is almost five. Compared to his little sister, he's incredibly evolved. He and Scamp are about the same age, reckoned in human years. Yet Aleksei, a mere kindergartner, evinces startling moments of conscience. He thinks about what makes the world tick. He concerns himself with profound matters such as motives and justice. He offers his little sister an extra strawberry. He is already his own authority. Up to a point. A point his mother, my friend Yelena, superbly understands. She's a kindergarten teacher, and more significantly, she's definitely a grown-up. As a grown-up, she can muster authority, both as a teacher, and as a parent. She knows that little children should not be expected to navigate complex decisions. For a toddler, even "vanilla or chocolate?" is a complex decision. Yet, in many households, school children rule the roost, their bidding reigns. They get their way. Without even a hint of discernment for what's right, either for them or for the situation, and with a genius for strategy and timing, they tyrannize their elders with an exquisite arsenal of whimpers, whines, pouts, tantrums, and other successful unpleasantries. Before long, as teenagers, they drive, drink, have babies, go to college, and know they are grown-ups. I certainly did, and to prove it got married at 19. Where are the grown-ups? What has enfeebled us? Why are we overwhelmed by our children?

Chapter Two

Training – More Than Potty

Scamp has reached the full potential of his education; for Aleksei, the process is just beginning. So why compare them? Isn't it offensive to compare a child to a dog? It is. There is no comparison. All I'm trying to say is that training is a necessary stage for both child and dog. The dog will never really outgrow his training, in spite of the anthropomorphic intelligence every dog owner attributes to his pet.

There are people who object to the word "training" in conjunction with human activities such as, say, the preparation of teachers. They object to "teacher training," preferring instead "teacher education." Dogs and horses, they rightfully say, are "trained." Only in the phrase "potty training" is "training" never questioned. "Potty education" is not a contender. Why? Because when it comes to matters of the body, or physical things in general, we agree that "training" is what's needed. Athletes are trained. Soldiers are trained. There's even such a thing as a training bra. You can train a plant; you can train your hair. And you certainly can, and this book is about the how and why of it, train a child. What's more, you can train a child without in the slightest impairing that child's unique potential.

Lucia is being potty trained. She is not yet verbal, apart from grunts and shouts that leave me clueless, but have linguistic content for her mom, Yelena, and her big brother Aleksei. Yet she communicates her wants flawlessly. She already understands everything her mom says to her. Slowly, she will be civilized, will learn not to poop any old time, will learn that you shouldn't start with the chocolate, will learn to offer her brother a bit of that brownie. Scamp has been trained not to poop any old time. He's learned to behave less like the ruffian he was, and more like the gentleman he's become, but language? Very limited. He astonishes me with his eloquent eyes, ears and tail, but he will never ever take the Scholastic Aptitude Test.

The very first entry for "train" as in "verb used with object" in my online dictionary[1] gives us a broad, and for our purposes, relevant definition with a telling example: to develop or form the habits, thoughts, or behavior of (a child or other person) by discipline and instruction: to train an unruly boy.

Habits! That's it. Potty training is about habits. My dog Scamp's training is ALL ABOUT HABITS. Transforming a toddler into a school child is ALL ABOUT HABITS.

Training is the means to an end, and the end is a newly acquired habit. A new habit can be so vexedly hard to acquire that we need to be in training to make it a habit. But beware the hard-earned habit. How quickly it ensnares us. We all know how grueling it is to kick a habit. Often we cannot kick hard enough to shake it loose. We become addicted. Even innocuous habits, like listening to the radio when we drive, annoy us if we want to assert our independence over them. Habits challenge us coming and going. They're hard to acquire and then harder to lose. Although a life without habits would be as much of a jumble as life without memory, life ruled by habit results in obsessive extremes. Do we rule the habits, or do they rule us, is the question that allows us to harness our habits to our purpose, and not theirs. It's a lifelong effort, because habits are sneaky. They harden and imprison us covertly. Military training, which inculcates habits deliberately to create soldiers trained to respond automatically no matter what, is effective but counter-productive for a human being's inner development. Training of habits needs thoughtful direction.

Most of the time, when we're talking about training a dog, or teaching a child manners, we're talking about habits of behavior. Yet our dictionary tells us that forming habits of thought is equally significant. Those are the invisible habits. Not undetectable, though. It goes without saying that other people's habits of thought, not my own, are the real culprits.

Do habits of behavior give rise to habits of thought? Do habits of thought engender morality? BIG questions. To me the answer is an unequivocal YES. We'll get to that later in the final chapter. For now, let's return to Scamp, for whom morality, as we've seen, is not an issue, and for whom habits were altogether alien when we met, so that teaching him new habits was an urgent need.

When I acquired him, he was loving and uncontrollable. He had only one way to communicate his puppy-affection: he nipped. He nipped with his four feet on the ground, and left a garter of blue welts around my thighs; he nipped while jumping up at me, and left bracelets of broken skin on my upper arms. This was not fun. When I walked him, he plunged forward, then lunged back to bite the leash. House breaking was not an issue, he seemed to have learned that in his orphanage days.

When I first saw him at the pet fair that bright September day, he was conspicuously calm. He stood quietly amidst a rough and tumble muddle of a dozen mutts yipping and nipping in their crowded pen. Reddish-blonde, short-haired, long-legged, floppy-eared, his long tail wagging gently . . . One of the handlers saw me staring at him – I suppose they are trained to recognize the smitten look – and suggested I take him for a walk. The handler accompanied us. We walked. The dog was demure. He did not tug. He did not pull. He did not bark. He trotted by my side as if he'd always been there, occasionally glancing up at me with his extraordinary amber eyes.

Having been an educator since my 20s, I just knew I'd be able to handle this docile dog with the beautiful eyes. I had a fenced in back yard and surely he'd be okay back there while I got the house organized for him.

"I'll take him," I said. Such is the nature of destined decisions. They make themselves spontaneously. I signed the papers, handed over a check, got the car, and got the dog home without incident.

And then the fun began.

Chapter Three

Getting Acquainted

His papers said he was a Kelpie, and about six months old. Honestly, I can't now remember how I got through the first 24 hours. I do remember that he charged through the house, knew no bounds, and loved me black and blue.

A friend brought over a dog crate. I put an old pillow in it. Scamp dragged the pillow out, ripped it apart, dug out the stuffing. He did not take to that crate. He was very persistent in making his dislike apparent. In the backyard, he chewed what he could, favoring grape vines. Irrigation tubing was irresistible. In the living room, table legs were appealing, as were rugs, books, and potted plants.

In short, I had got myself a pretty wild dog. Why this crazy creature had acted with such sweetness and docility when I first met him at the pet fair remains a mystery. Drugged? Overwhelmed? Karmically disposed? Whatever. When we got home, he went nuts!

Turning desperately to YouTube for instruction, I came across this memorable injunction:

If your dog does something stupid, roll up a newspaper and bash yourself on the head. It's always your fault.

Why did this sound so familiar? How often had I made similar, if less graphic, remarks to novice teachers of children! **Look to yourself; Don't blame the kids.**

About the time that the dog, who started out as a very naughty boy and whom I aptly named Scamp, had been civilized, so that his sweet nature emerged in his pleasing demeanor as my faithful companion, eager to learn and obey commands and able to anticipate my every move, I was mentoring various first grade teachers. It was this conjunction, the "civilizing" of Scamp and the work these teachers faced in "civilizing" their young charges, that engendered this book.

Although the examples that follow come from life in the classroom, they also are applicable to life at home. Teachers and parents have very different roles in the raising of children. Their relationship to their charges is incomparable. Even so, when it comes to the children's behavior, the two realms overlap instructively.

Why, I wondered, as I observed many a struggling teacher, is it so difficult to acquaint school children with classroom procedures and rules? Raise your hand. Take out your crayons. Let's form a line. The teacher is well-meaning, the children mean no harm, yet orderly silence is rare, and chaos, like a growling beast, ominously threatens most of the time. It's a beast that resists prodding, resists humor, resists punishment; a beast with 19 or 34 adorable little heads. The fledgling teachers I was asked to help were often ragged with the effort of making themselves heard above the rumble. Sometimes, just for a calm interlude, I took myself to the beneficent atmosphere of a seasoned teacher's class, where the routine was established and everyone was moving forward in a sunny mood through a clearly structured lesson.

My work as director of a teacher training didn't preclude ongoing stints teaching in grade schools. "The children," I'd tell the grown-up teachers-in-training, "keep me honest." Being a school teacher was an essential, if peripheral, part of my work with future teachers, novice teachers, practicum teachers, apprentice teachers, ineffective, despairing, not-in-charge-of-their-charges teachers. I was often asked to mentor or evaluate teachers, and usually, by the time I was called in to put out a brush fire, the problems were already crackling fiercely.

When I first started teaching I was a green 26, barely older than my slouchy high school students. Those teenagers were intimidating with their knowing noses in the air. They confused me. Now, four decades down the line, I have the authority of experience and gray hair. Often, when advising green teachers, pale parents, or teachers-in-training shaking in their boots, I had the temerity to admonish them: **Look to yourself; Don't blame the kids**. For most adults, this is unwelcome news. It had certainly been unwelcome news in my teaching infancy. I blamed those teenagers all the time. Yet here was YouTube offering the very same advice, but for a dog, a dog who

was causing me as much grief as any stubborn three-year-old, any sullen adolescent can cause the grown-ups.
In my living room, I had an old chair of sentimental as well as practical value. It had been in my mother's room at the old age home where she eventually died. It was no longer pristine, but it was very comfortable. It was a recliner without a lever mechanism. To make the chair horizontal, you simply leaned back. So satisfying! Furthermore, it had a small footprint, taking up little space. How it happened I don't know, but about a week after Scamp arrived, I walked into my living room and found one arm of this chair with its "bones" showing. Scamp had chewed through the upholstery down to the wood.

Luckily I'd removed the big carpets before he got to them, but he managed to use various cushions, throw rugs, towels, table legs, and a pair of gardening clogs as teething rings.

It was all very well to say I should roll up a newspaper and hit myself on the head – I was willing to do that – only I didn't see how that would improve Scamp's waywardness.

I Googled "kelpie" and found inspiration:

They do not respond to harsh or heavy-handed methods. Training should be done with **firmness, fairness, and consistency**.

Of course! Here was a basic pedagogical tenet: Children "do not respond to harsh or heavy-handed methods." They do respond to **"firmness, fairness, and consistency"**. I already knew that. Now I needed to adapt the decades of my classroom work to canine parameters.

But then a strange thing happened. The dog brought me to my heels. He made me pull up my socks. His relatively simple requirements bared the essentials. They were the very essentials that those teachers needed to master. The question remained, though, what exactly was the training to look like?

That's what Scamp helped crystallize out of my forty-five years of teaching.

Chapter Four

A Child Is Not a Dog

Let's get one thing perfectly clear. I am NOT saying that a child and a dog are congruent or even similar. They don't have all that much in common, really. A child will evolve beyond the capacities of a dog in an awesomely short time. No matter how old Scamp gets, he will never understand my rapture as we cross the Golden Gate Bridge. What I'm looking to demystify is how to avoid having to hit yourself over the head with that rolled up newspaper.

When the baby stands up, s/he succeeds in overcoming one of nature's greatest forces: gravity. Learning to walk is an awesome accomplishment, an enormous task executed without anyone's help, a solo achievement, an act of supreme self-reliance. Sure, parents can encourage, chairs can support, but in the end, a human baby, nothing daunted, practices, practices, practices, and finally gets it right all alone. Scamp and all his kin walk a whole lot sooner. The colt famously wobbles onto four spindly legs within hours of birth. But the horizontal gait of the horse will never compare in achievement to the child's vertical conquest of gravity.

Then, too, when the toddler says "Mama," a moment every parent relishes, s/he initiates the supremely complex process toward literacy that no dog, no animal in fact, will ever accomplish. Scamp communicates, but his language must remain wordless and primitive. He has a wide range of throaty sounds, but he is inarticulate. He is sentenceless. Grammar doesn't concern him. Nor is he interested in nuance. Desire is what he expresses best. "I want" comprises the greatest part of his expressive universe. I can read his eyes, the tilt of his head, the wag of his tail. I can see whether he wants water, wants to be petted, wants me to play with him. Being a sentient and domesticated creature, he knows fear, joy, pain, sadness and can give voice to them with his growl, bark, and whine. He is eloquent for a dog. I can hear whether his bark means a little fear or a lot, but he will never be able to explain anything, least of all himself. A four-year-old human, on the other hand, is already preternaturally articulate, often poetically so.

Case in point: I was talking to Aleksei a little while ago. I was over at Yelena and Michael's for dinner and had read Aleksei his bedtime story. When I closed the book he quietly said, "That's not very good." And I had to agree with him. He wasn't expressing a literary opinion, he was commenting on character. The people in the book were not very good. By the time a child is about three, he already comprehends a good deal about the nature of life and the world. At almost five, Aleksei has a bead on morality; by 28, some self-knowledge may begin to arise; by middle age wisdom is not impossible. Whereas: the wisdom in my fine pooch was his from birth and will never exceed the grasp of his ears, eyes, and snout.

Aleksei's younger sister, two-year-old Lucia, comprehends abstractions. She asks for her ragged cloth rabbit, even when it's in the room next-door. She gets the concept of cause and effect. She knows that stamping her feet gets her mother's attention. Scamp too knows the signals. Hand in pocket, for example, means treat on the way. While I was reading to her brother, Lucia brought me her beloved threadbare rabbit doll; Scamp will bring me his rope toy when he wants to play. Lucia overturned a box of blocks, just as supper was ready, in a show of self-determined obstreperousness; Scamp will race off the trail and onto the street, to follow the irresistible scent of an open compost pile. He is jealous when I give my attention to a voice on the phone; Lucia wormed her way into my lap as I read to Aleksei. When I sit here at this keyboard for too long, Scamp comes over and butts my elbow with his head to dislodge me. He can be silly, deliberately obtuse (the terrible twos syndrome), or cuddly as a lap dog. Every mother knows how fleeting this stage of mostly sweet self-assertion is. In Scamp, it is permanent. He will age, and grow more feeble and less able, but fundamentally, what I've got is what I've got; whereas a child is perplexingly inconstant. The metamorphosis of the child as it "grows up" is, to say the least, mind-boggling.

The first hours after the birth of a child ring in a set of changes so overwhelming, that being overwhelmed is expected of new parents. Lovingly, they dote with fascination upon every gurgle, burp, and poop. As the months pass, the day-to-day changes become less noticeable. Year-to-year, though, change becomes apparent. By the time the child enters first grade, the mewling, puking, burping, pooping infant has been transformed beyond recognition. Individually each child is in a constant state of metamorphosis, yet each age has its distinct signature.

I like to guess a child's age. Are those basketball players on the schoolyard 7th or 8th graders? Is that a five- or a six-year-old skipping through the supermarket aisles? When you see a child every day, little seems to change. Sometimes, though, the slow metamorphosis accelerates. Puberty announces itself unmistakably and soul changes during adolescence are epiphanous. Will there be changes again as the high school student enters college, graduates, enters the labor force, weds, has offspring? Certainly. But such change as can be effected after college is the result of hard inner work, which the self-help industry, in all its obvious and subtle manifestations from aerobics to AA, knows, as it caters to the challenge of self-transformation. If it took as much effort to make a child grow physically, as it takes to grow a teenager into a mature adult, every parent of a pre-school child would have to exchange his or her profession for full-time child-rearing. Of course that's nonsense, because no one knows how to make a child grow, any more than anyone knows how the daffodils in my back yard grow. I mean actually grow. Actually get bigger. Growth in its many variables – physical, biological, spiritual, – is still, ultimately, a mystery. So whereas every child gets bigger, grows older, grows wiser, matures from day to day, a dog, even Scamp, soon reaches a plateau and stays there. Scamp is at the level of a two-year-old, and there he'll stay until he declines. Boasting that a dog can distinguish among 100 objects cannot hold a candle to the subtle soul perceptions that a two-year-old already experiences.

Like the two year old, Scamp is motivated by results. He is a smart cookie. In fact, the promise of any treat raises his IQ immediately. If he knows you have a treat in your pocket, Scamp can do algebra. Such civilizing as has taken hold of him (Sit! Lie! Wait! Stay! Jump! Heel! Fetch! Drop it! Leave it! Come!) was motivated by the promise of a treat. Call it cause and effect, or call it bribery. It works wonders for dogs, and, please don't take offense, it works wonders in infants, toddlers, and in school. Nor does it take long for even the newest of newborns to grasp the formula: If . . . then. If I cry, then Mommy comes. The baby knows this, and mom and dad now need to learn how to reverse the flow, or, in other words, how to, dare we say it, train the child.

The trick is that the expectation must be in keeping with the child's developmental capacities. And what a thorny topic that is.

Knowing what is intrinsic to the creature you're dealing with is key. Cruelty yields spectacular results, but spectacular results are not the goal. When I was a school child in colonial South Africa, corporeal goads were the norm. Even I, the good little girl that I was, got rapped on the knuckles with a wooden ruler. It didn't hurt, but the grown-ups lost credibility. Did they think I was going to do better because of it? Whipping an animal is equally primitive. Not statistical results, but self-sustained behavior that can grow with the child should be the goal. Are we grown-up enough to cultivate behavior sufficient to create a workable environment, so that in the classroom we can get along and learn how to learn, and in the home fear doesn't reign impiously? In my home, Scamp and I can now coexist in mutually satisfying conditions. A dog who insists on nipping is undesirable. A dog who is all instinct and no culture is a hazard. He will create chaos. A classroom driven by the constant disorder of shouting children, or, worse, a shouting teacher, will not yield education. Forcing order through an inhuman, or an inhumane regime, will, inexorably, traumatize children or pets.

Scamp has reached the upper limit of his education. We human beings try to foist our measure of intelligence on the animal world. We celebrate the "language" of whales, gorillas, and dogs. Better we celebrated the true nature of these creatures, which is intrinsically bound up with their animal bodies, their natural instincts. The vaunted canine nose is more intelligent that any human nose will ever be, but basset hounds cannot help being sniffing prodigies. Their olfactory apparatus has been bred into them. They are smell specialists. Their snout is an inhuman tool. There are humans who suffer from hypersensitivity to scents. They require "fragrance free" zones. But their sensitivity is an aberration, whereas a dog's olfactory sensitivity is inherent. We humans are generalists when it comes to our five senses. We don't see as well as a hawk, or hear as well as an owl. Even with extreme training we'll never sprint like a jaguar, swim like a sardine, or leap like a lemur. Instead, we can both create and find pleasure in music and art, and, more humanly than anything else, we can find joy in sacrifice and love.

Although Renaissance universality is no longer an ideal in our mouse-driven age of byte-sized specializations, we are, as human beings, capable of vast complexities of thought, feeling, and action that thoroughly eclipse all animal performance. Even dog agility competitions, for all their amazing athleticism, require human direction. Scamp can smell a peanut at the far end of Drake's beach, but it's simply in his nature. It's not a talent he's honed. It's not the result of training. In no way was education part of his snout's sensitivities. Yes, humans have learned to exploit the canine's nose, the camel's stride, the hawk's talons, the equine's hoofs. Yes, individual pets take on their individual human's wants, moods, and expectation to astonishing degrees. But the limitation of every species' achievements lies in the very fact that realization of its species innate potential is the only possible goal. Whereas a child's potential is never known, the limits of a dog's potential are pedigreed. Will Aleksei become a pilot or a gardener? Will his sister become a bookbinder or an engineer? Who's to say? Their parents certainly haven't a clue.

Chapter Five

Pedigree or Pedagogue

If you want to determine which breed of dog is the one for you, whether it's an Affenpinscher or a Yorkshire Terrier, you can turn to a shopping list of dog attributes or scroll through 180+ dog breeds to learn all about their "traits, characteristics and general behavior."

The point is: YOU CAN DECIDE EXACTLY WHAT YOU WANT, AND GET IT. Stud fees prove it. That is NOT how it works with children, even in our genetically modified designer world.

Although humans do now "shop" for offspring, the individual human being is still a mystery that no amount of genetic expectation can anticipate. You don't know exactly what you're getting. You may know something about how the child will look, but the child will be its own self, able to surprise you endlessly. Able, eventually, to surprise even him or herself. Individuality is the telling signature of a human being, as the three sets of twins in the last 7th grade I taught, attest. One set was identical, and even they were entirely dissimilar in their "traits, characteristics and general behavior." Even ordinary siblings, born of the same parents and raised in the same environment, can flummox their parents with their differences.

Such differences, announcing the unique potential within each child, require freedom to develop and emerge. Reducing that freedom, by suppressing what lives in the individual, is a rampant temptation for anyone looking for a shortcut to enforcing habits. Uniforms, teams, standardized tests . . . we think nothing of subjecting children to these modes of uniformity, and in moderation, such generic deployments can be benign. Their opposite, anarchy, is certainly not a remedy. And when a human being is reduced to being a number, a cipher, an indistinguishable member of a category, humanity is attacked. Were we to write about a race, any race, with the zoological objectivity appropriate to the description of any animal species, we would be committing a crime against humanity. Humanity as a whole is not yet convinced of this, and that's the basis of so much trouble. Sociology has tried to sanction such descriptions, and has usually succeeded only in cases where the object of its research was not able to defend itself. We are offended by racism, unless we as human beings are not properly human. Reducing a human's individuality, is, therefore, the first goal of fascism. Whereas it's easy to distinguish the differences among dogs by breed, human individuality trumps any group.

Dogs, on the contrary, are bred NOT to surprise; uniformity wins Best in Show.

No one would confuse a Labrador retriever with a Chihuahua. You don't find Chihuahuas as guide dogs for the blind. The very word, "breed" implies generic characteristics. By nature, a human being, whatever the heritage, is a world unto him or herself.

The American Kennel Club offers competitive shows for over 180 breeds. Each breed is judged according to a template of the ideal. There's a word for this: "Conformation."

In a dog conformation show, judges aren't merely comparing the dogs to each other. Rather, they judge each dog against the parameters of the idealized version of its breed. In other words, when the judge looks at your poodle, Fluffy, he is comparing Fluffy to the written standards of the ideal poodle. The standards address various body parts and attributes. [2]

So if it's a Fluffy you want, you can get one. You can decide exactly which breed suits your needs and circumstances, and get it. I didn't know exactly what I was getting when I got Scamp, but I knew what I was not getting. I was not getting Fluffy.

We humans tend to anthropomorphize our pets. We call them domestic pets because we domesticate them, meaning, we humanize them to a limited, and what I'm trying to say is that it's a VERY limited, extent. We even write books about them as individuals! Yet the ideal of an animal, even an animal as domesticated as the dog, is a template. Conformation is all. So we have it coming and going. The perfect cocker spaniel conforms to a recognized template, "an ideal version of its breed," while as every cocker spaniel owner knows, there's only one of its kind. Books and movies about individual animals are enduringly popular because of that very dichotomy. We love to see an animal lifted out of its template. Black Beauty, Lassie, Big Red, and all the other stories I so loved as a child, are mostly anthropomorphized accounts. In some cases, especially when filmmakers enter the arena of the wild animals, they obscure the generic quality of the animals by giving them names, and cleverly manipulating the footage into a "personalized" story. In reality, a herd of impala on the plains of Africa does not consist of individuals, nor does the flock of black birds fluting on the wires in fall.

When humans subjugate their own uniqueness, their own one-of-a-kind disposition and standing in the world; when they band together in cliques, gangs, armies; professions, unions, hobbies; skin colors, languages, nations, and regions, then they fundamentally do violence to their greatest attribute, their own rarity. Of course humans need family, friends, community. But once they identify with uniform, traditions, rituals, or lose themselves in any mass and become mindless, then the troubles start. That's the sort of identification that teenagers ascribe to, and which social media has so brilliantly exploited. They are resorting to identity by herd, flock, gaggle, swarm; throng, mob, rabble, gang. It's not a grown-up thing to do.

When these teens were babies, they all looked a lot alike. Newborns are given name tags so that one doesn't get mixed up with another. Newborns still have a generic look. Even in first grade, there is still a somewhat generic aspect to the children. Little Jessica's parents might consider that to be a mighty insult, and for Jessica's parents Jessica is unique. It's indisputable that Jessica *is* unique. And her uniqueness is still somewhat unexpressed. She is a little girl with promise. Whatever her obstacles and limitations in first grade, we have no way of knowing what her life's achievements will be. Therein lies the endless fascination of biography: the unpredictability of life's arc. It's a human attribute to be able to rise above circumstances, to live to tell the tale, as so many autobiographies do.

"The child," wrote William Wordsworth famously, "is father of the man." True enough (especially if we add, "mother of the woman"). Glimpses of a child's future do often flash toward us, but a human's range of opportunity, web of possibility, flux of conditions, unforeseeable reach of inspirations, kaleidoscopic complexity of kismet – all these exceed the best of guesses most of the time. The ideal upbringing allows a child to grow into the one and only adult she will become. Instead, so often, categories, templates, expectations, fill-in-the-blank evaluations determine a child's future. The abolition of the screamingly inappropriate No Child Left Behind acknowledges the futility of standardized testing, just one of the limiting straitjackets so much of our educational systems rely on.

Human beings have infinite promise. Their education can help them toward the self-education that is their birthright, and which no dog can ever achieve.

Have you ever waited for a familiar face on a bustling street corner? How do you recognize that face? Considering the dearth of features in the human face – two eyes, one nose, one mouth – the variety is magnificent. Even when we take the whole body into consideration, there might be aberrations, identifying peculiarities, but fundamentally, the variety is limited. There are NOT 180 different looks to human physiology. Just think about what our world would be like if there were. That's a fantasy world à la Star Trek inhabited by the likes of Cardassians, Romulans, Klingons, Vulcans, not to mention generations of aliens, etc. To accommodate the Star Trek vision, human faces were pinched and pulled and distorted until a distinctly inhuman visage was shaped. Here on earth, though, one human face is not that unlike the next. Nevertheless, and almost inexplicably if you've ever waited for someone at an airport, the myriad strangers huffing past you makes no impression, whereas the one you're waiting for is instantly recognizable.

So, physically, there is not all that much to distinguish us. We are, as a species, not as different from one another as a dachshund is from a husky. True, we fall into groups, many determined by environment. If you live south of the Alps, you'll likely have a different disposition from your uncle to the north. But all those cultural and geographical variations such as skin color, race, tribe, religion, language, weather, food, etc. don't account for personal heroism, idealism, creativity, insight, kindness, morality, etc. When we "fall upon the thorns of life" and then get up to continue the quest, we're striving into our own future in spite of the limitations of the group. Therein lies the genesis of true self-education, of inner growth. That's something Scamp can't manage.

Chapter Six

Firmness, Fairness, and Consistency; Practice and Repetition

Last fall, I spent some time in Wales, where border collies are ubiquitous. I got curious, and landed on a YouTube video in which an old man, a veteran sheep dog trainer, describes an early exercise. For three weeks (*three weeks!*), the four-month-old puppy is simply made to circle a small enclosure in which some half dozen sheep are milling about. The puppy is learning to circle around the sheep, but a fence separates him from them. He is learning to follow the command: circle this way, circle that way. "You can really only work the dog for 10 minutes a day. After that a young dog loses concentration."

Well, I thought, here's a born teacher, and no wonder he's been so successful at training dogs.

He was **firm, fair, and consistent** in his handling of the pups. He didn't have overly high expectations. He repeated and repeated. And there's the key: **repetition**.

Usually it's the adult who tires of the repetition, not the children. Children are, fundamentally, conservative. They like repetition. They love to hear the story again. And woe unto you if you leave out a detail or change a word. When their regular teacher is out, they tell their substitute teacher how it's done. "We don't do it like that," is a familiar whine when a substitute teacher steps into a class. Of course, I'm talking about young children, though even older children prefer to keep things as they are.

Take Lizzy, for example: I met her just after she was born. Whenever I was a guest in her home around bedtime, the same routine would be in place. It included my favorite moment, when both parents stood by her bed and quietly said goodnight to all that Lizzy had encountered that day, including the sun and trees, grass and clouds; but also the people. For good measure, distant relatives were named each night. It was a litany. Lizzy listened raptly. The recall of the day was concluded with a simple lullaby. Just one verse. A lullaby that assured Lizzy that in the morning she would find all as she had left it the night before.

Lizzy is grown-up now. I'm sure that the repetition of so many routines of her childhood – bedtime was just one of them – helped make her the energetic, dependable woman she is today.

Lizzy's parents had the strength of their convictions, and the endurance to patiently repeat the routine night after night. They enjoyed it. It gave them a chance to focus, to think back on the day. They kept it up until Lizzy was in 6th grade. That's longer than we might have expected such a ritual to be effective, and that's my point. When a child knows the routine, knows what to expect, lives in the comfort and certainty of habit and routine, security for life is fostered. Parents can make that happen.

The classroom and home are playing fields where rules, or habits, are necessary. There are many players, and without some basic regulations, chaos would ensue. A classroom is a community where rules are expedient. Everyone's job is easier if there are a few basic rules. The trick is how to keep the rules alive, how to keep the rules useful, practical, organic, and pliable. An organic rule is one that has grown out of the needs of the situation, unlike a gratuitous rule, which is illogical, pedantic, superimposed on the situation, and counter-productive. An organic rule ought to be pliable enough to adapt to the growing situation. It ought to change the way a tree in a forest adapts to its environment. Military rules are not organic. They are notoriously rigid. They formalize hierarchy. They achieve control. They are gratuitous. Gratuitous rules antagonize and hinder; organic rules expedite and galvanize.

"Rule" is not a useful word in the world of first graders. You can't really explain it to a seven-year old anymore than I could explain the importance of "Sit!" to Scamp. For both dog and first grader, a rule is a total abstraction, its wisdom beyond comprehension. It just has to be done, habitually. If little Gregory in the first grade understood the importance of raising a hand to be called on, he would most likely do it.

You can explain yourself black and blue to first graders. Unless they've developed habits, "habits of operation," they will revert to their natural anything-goes and I'm-the-most-important-person-here inclinations. Habit is key. Habits have to be trained, the way a vine has to be trained. Neither the vine nor the child will succeed if they flop all over and their scraggly tendrils are left to their own devices. Training requires constancy and consistency. Ask anyone training for a marathon. Ask anyone training (or practicing, which is training) for an audition. Self-administered discipline, or discipline administered by a coach will get you to the Olympics or to Carnegie Hall. In first grade, where motivation and ambition or talent are not yet catalysts for the 6- or 7-year-old trainee's self-discipline, it's up to the teacher to foster the habits that buttress the rules.

Playing the violin is completely unnatural. Look at what those hands have to learn to do. If it were natural, I could play the violin and so could you. Talent helps, but that old adage, "How do you get to Carnegie Hall? Practice! Practice! Practice!" is the truth. There's no way around it. In my 20s, when I hung out with conservatory graduates, six hours of practice a day was not uncommon. Okay, our first graders needn't practice their habits with that much ferocity. But it's not a bad idea to practice good habits. I mean, actually practice.

Let's say you are trying to teach the universal raise-your-hand-to-be-called-on rule. It should be practiced in as many possible ways as you can come up with. Invent a game in which hands must be raised. Tell a story and have everyone raise a hand every time you say the word "the" or whatever. Or every time you mention a color. Or every time you mention a name. Nothing hard. Now you practice this until it's clear that every child gets the idea. This might take a lot longer than you think. Every time you name an animal. Every time you name a tree. Just keep it simple, and don't let the example overwhelm the point of the game, which is to raise your hand. Now you move from the raucous raising of hands to the quiet raising of hands. How to do this? This is where you need an imagination. I would try to embed the quiet raising of hands in a different set of actions, a sort of Simon Says approach. How many ways can we raise a hand. Standing? Facing the back of the room? Raising both hands? Raising one hand quietly? Once you've achieved the last one with some consistency (which, again, could take a week or more – remember we are "practicing" this no more than 5 or so minutes a day), you can start there, and use whatever worked to make that happen, that is, do whatever got the right Simon Says response, and then ask the children to use that particular way of doing it for your next practice session story, which could involve raising-a-hand-quietly every time you ask a question in the story, or every time you say a word that begins with "T." Now we could tell an interactive story, where the children do answer questions, but of course, only after they raise a hand quietly. Finally, at last, this particular habit is leached into the habit life of the class. Now the grown-up has to insist on it. One exception and chaos erupts as everyone calls out.

Does this classroom example translate into life at home? Yes, it does. Teachers are not parents, but parents are teachers. *You Are Your Child's First Teacher* by Rahima Baldwin Dancy clearly makes that point. At home, the child learns to eat with a fork, learns not to interrupt, learns, learns, learns. And if the parent can implement the slow, incremental approach to habit-teaching, and can insist with a modicum of rigor, success will be achieved with far less stress for both parent and child.

In school as well as at home, the sequence needs to be analyzed, and broken down into steps, like a recipe. The task of the coach is to heed the recipe, to keep the sequence intact, to prevent the delusion and false expectations of short cuts. Slow incremental steps are the recipe for success in almost any endeavor, but slow, incremental steps require discipline. At first such discipline is easier to achieve with a coach or teacher. Ultimately though, a teacher should become superfluous. Here we have one of the mighty distinctions between teachers and parents. It's a distinction that is painful for both.

Very few people succeed on talent alone. The people with talent who succeed are usually the ones who harness their talent through training, practice, and plain hard work. A first grader will adapt to hard work much more enthusiastically if it comes in the guise of a game, without fear of failure. Then it can be improved upon by plain hard work, which for young children at school or at home, consists of practice. Or in other words: Repetition. Consistency.

It's up to the teacher or parent, the trainer, to insist on the consistency by means of repetition. How can you be sure you can consistently hit the ball if you don't try to hit it repeatedly? It goes without saying. A budding violinist practices the scales to achieve consistency. If you're a teacher, you'll undo any step forward when you call on someone who hasn't raised a hand. The children, by nature, will be inconsistent with the rule. But you, the teacher, have to find a creative way to insist on consistency. If the children don't follow the rule, roll up a newspaper and hit yourself on the head. You might want the entire Sunday Times under your desk. Because first graders are geniuses at making you forget your own rule. If little Julia, who is shy and retiring and rarely raises her hand, blurts out the answer, what does it take to say, "Raise your hand, Julia"? It takes the absolute conviction that **consistency** is not an abstraction. Now look, it's a foregone conclusion that teaching is an art, and art consists of knowing when to break the rules, so in the case of Julie, you need to use your own intuition. I'm just saying, most of the time, we err on the side of inconsistency. Take another all too common case: Tony, who is loud and brash and smart, already knows how to read. Again and again, while a classmate is struggling to pronounce the word on the blackboard, Tony will thrust his hand in the air and without being called on will yell out. What now?

Tony knows a consequence is justified. He knows he shouldn't yell out. But, he is enthusiastic, and he is quick, and he is loud. He yells out the answer. When you think of it, this business of raising your hand to be called on is distinctly an acquired habit. It is contrary to instinct. It requires cultivation. It is one of the hardest things to learn, to wait one's turn. If I know the answer, why shouldn't I yell it out? At home no one minds when I do that, in fact, at home I get smiles when I yell out the right answer. Ah, but here at school Tony is not alone, and Tony, shrewd as he is, already has complete mastery of what is fair. So a consequence for Tony's yelling out is appropriate. But it must be an appropriate consequence. (More on that later.) The point is, there has to be a consequence, and this consequence has to be consistent. It has to be administered to everyone, Tony AND Julia, impartially. That's being **fair.**

That's the nature of training. Scamp and I have walked through my front door about 2,555 times. For about 2,000 of these exits, I have reminded Scamp that he has to sit before I open the door. He knows this, but he doesn't anticipate it. With my hand on the doorknob, I wait until he sits. Then I open the door, and he waits for the signal before he walks out. It's a practical sequence, because it gives me a chance to make sure that Tuli, my cat, is not lounging about outside just beyond the front door where Scamp will feint an attack, or that a neighbor isn't walking a dog past the driveway, because either of these scenarios would terrify either the cat or the neighbor. So this morning, our 2,556th time through the door, I had to remind him yet again, to sit, and only then did I open the door. Pedantic? You betcha! But my dog and I walk serenely down the driveway, without any hysteria, and that's my preference. Furthermore, after he sits to wait for the door to be opened, the demure, patient, expectant look on his face is priceless. He likes to wait for the moment when he's allowed to cross the threshold. He has a special way of sitting when he's waiting like that. I never see him sit like that at any other time, one front foot elegantly in front of the other.

So when a teacher, eager to encourage a student, eager to hear the right answer, is inconsistent about the raise-your-hand-to-be-called-on expectation, she ought to roll up a newspaper and hit herself on the head.

The exhausting aspect of consistency is that it requires consistency about what to be consistent about.

Do we expect silence when we line up? Do we expect chairs pushed under tables when we leave the desks? Do we expect no hats in class? We need to pick our fights, and then be 100% consistent. Or if there are exceptions, they should be ours to decide, not passive reactions to the exception.

When Scamp doesn't sit down as we leave the house, I simply don't open the door. What will the first grade teacher do if the lunchtime murmur becomes a thunderous rumble? The one thing that is utterly useless is to do anything that exacerbates the problem. So for the teacher to yell, when the children are yelling, is just counter-productive. For the teacher to ignore a child who has not raised a hand simply weakens the need for the rule. And here's what's so pernicious. It may take three weeks to learn how to do it right, but it takes only one exception to undo all that work.

I used to teach 5th through 12th grade German. I did that for five years, and by the third year I realized that the less English I spoke in the classroom, the more real the need for the foreign language became. By speaking the foreign language, and doing things in the foreign language, whether recitation of poetry, or singing, games, or arithmetic, you build up a foreign-language-edifice. Then little Kevin gets annoyed at a neighbor and admonishes him in English, and the whole carefully constructed foreign-language structure comes tumbling down. Or you, the teacher, want to be sure the children understand the grammar, and give the instruction for the dative in English. Crash! Down come your labors. Now you have to start from the foundation again, and build up that foreign-language edifice layer by layer. These days, this idea is called "immersion." Whatever you call it, one exception to the rule lays waste the effort of days.

Chapter Seven

The Need for Objectivity

Before children come to first grade, many of them have attended some form of pre-school. Lucky the child whose pre-school experience is not academic. More and more educators agree that "play is the child's work," and that play is the desired modus for a child in kindergarten.

Left to their own devices, children "play at" whatever they witness in their surroundings, thus the popularity of dolls and cars, daggers, guns, cloaks and make-believe food. There are also the imaginary worlds, unrelated to daily life, that children are so good at constructing. Lucky the child whose own forces of imagination have not been decimated by pre-packaged digital fare. A wooden stick can be an airplane; a sandbox can become an intricate engineering project, especially when water is involved; a bush can be a fort. In such activities, pre-school children ought to be allowed to be children, and the only rules they need follow are those required by their habitat and safety. Running after a ball into the street is not allowed. Neither is using the stick airplane to bash a playmate.

So civilizing influences have to exist before first grade. When you get right down to it, civilizing influences exist the instant the child is born. At first, instinct suffices for bodily needs. The child uses physical expression, it cries, to express physical needs: hunger, thirst, diaper change and so on. But soon more than metabolic needs assert themselves. The child wants and needs attention. Not just the body needs attention. The soul too must be attended. Loneliness, fear, anger: these have their own language. Moms and sometimes Dads can take one look and see what is inwardly moving the child. But whereas physical neglect is no parent's choice, the child's emotional demands require tempering. The terrible twos are terrible just because the child must learn to adjust to the needs of others on the planet. Here flourish seeds of future discontent, whether of the child or the parent. For sometimes, a child's imperious demands must be ignored. And what child is not imperious? It only takes one crying child on board to turn a pleasant flight into an operatic extravagance. Every passenger is held hostage, for reason does not apply. Certainly not to the child, and sometimes not even to the parent. In restaurants and other public spaces such as shops, swimming pools, busses, etc. the drama of the "naughty" child is common enough. But why is the child carrying on? The nearest adult needs to roll up a newspaper and thump herself on the head. The child has not been taught how to be in public. Publicly accepted behavior varies by geography: country, language, local culture determine the norm. So do extreme conditions. But I'm really talking about "normal" life with average parents and your average child.[3] When a child screams in public, something is already out of whack. Fundamentally, the child has learned through experience, that this is the way to get what it wants. When you really look at unwanted behavior in a child, it is almost always about the child's getting what it wants. Even teenagers who do crazy things are looking for recognition of something in them that no one in their life has seen. High jinks are basically a *cri de coeur.*

What then could be more counter-productive than responding positively to negative cues? And what is harder for Mom and Dad than resisting a child's tears?

This brings us to the big "O" word: Objectivity. In this realm, the puppy handler, the dog trainer, has a mighty advantage. He is not – by definition – in a subjective relationship to the critter. We love our dogs, but no matter how attached we are to them and they to us, they are not flesh of our flesh. It is just a fact. Scamp's antics, when they are counter-productive, require appropriate disciplinary measures. This is not as easy is it should be, because when he prances about in a fit of joy at the possibility of a car ride, and in his enthusiasm knocks the vase off the table, it's really not a good idea to let him into the car before he's registered my displeasure. Inevitably, the mini-drama will play out when I'm running late. How often have I praised him for the wrong thing? Times without counting. He comes when I whistle and his reward is in my hand, and I'm so happy that he's come when I whistled that I forget that I never give him a treat unless he sits first.

Parents continually find themselves in this bind. The child is nagging. The Mom promises a treat. The child continues to nag. The Mom provides the treat. The child registers: nag = treat. Children of two or three are geniuses at weakening their parents' resolve. They seem to know with calm conviction that it's their childish will against ours, and because you are the grown-up, and thus feel responsible for the little one, their will prevails more often than not. A child's will has a lot of fizz in it, like an unopened soda can, whereas the will of your average adult is comparatively stale, and the child gets that picture pretty quickly. Dinnertime, food in general, is a favorite platform. How many middle-class dinner table dramas have I witnessed? Scores. My relatively sheltered life did not include starving children. And although no child engaged in bourgeois mealtime drama has ever been in danger of starving, parents of a pouting child become pudding in the face of the child's culinary likes and dislikes. The parents cater to the child's whims. The child has trained them to do so, because it's so awfully difficult to be harsh with flesh of your flesh, especially when you fear the child's growling stomach. Hence the fabled step-mother. Her step-child is not flesh of her flesh, and thus she is liberated from the tyranny of subjectivity. Yet, without such subjectivity, any mom runs the danger of violating the child's innocent expectation that grown-ups are good people.

Childhood is a long process. Unlike goat kids that dance down steep precipices within days of birth, the human child is helpless for a long time. During those years of innocent expectation, the child depends on the subjectivity of its parents. In the average benign situation, the parents will want to minister to the child to the best of their ability. Yet helpless as the child is, he or she quickly adjusts to the ways of the world, and discovers how to press the parents' buttons. Once that happens, if the parent is unaware of the child's prowess in that direction, bad habits spawn like tadpoles. At the beginning of the child's life, the baby's tyrannous habits are self-preserving. The child's ability to cry to express its needs is welcome. The child cries and gets fed. There's so much guesswork in parenting a new-born, that any cue is a relief. But ever so quickly, the child takes advantage. As well it should. The grown-up, on the other hand, needs to apply some **OBJECTIVITY**. Is it really a good idea for the child to have another cookie? The child certainly thinks so.

Every time I feed Scamp I remind myself that he really is getting enough to eat, even though he is always starving. Dog owners congregating in dog parks will talk about this ravenous-dog behavior. There are theories. "It's their wolf ancestry," or "He was a shelter dog and didn't get fed enough as a pup." The bottom line, though, is that "they're always hungry." It's difficult but not impossible for me to realize as I feed him mornings and evenings that, although the half a cup of kibble supplemented in the mornings by two tablespoons of ground turkey looks marginal, the dog is in prime shape. Our last visit to the vet earned me praise for having a dog of perfect weight for his size. But because

I'm forever fretting about my own weight, I'm weighed down by my nagging doubts about the quantities for the dog.

The point is that it's a whole lot easier being the objective grown-up when you're in charge of a dog than when you're the Mom. It's in the nature of being a mom, blood-related, to fall into the bossy child syndrome. Sometimes, though, even dog owners fall prey to the bossy dog syndrome.

In some countries, dog training classes are compulsory. What do dog training classes provide? They provide training for the dog owners. The dog goes to school, and the dog owner is educated. Because even when the dog "gets" it, if the dog owner doesn't practice **CONSISTENCY**, all the training at school is out the window.

Something similar happens when the child goes to "school." Whether it's nursery, kindergarten, or child care of some other kind, the child will be in the care of someone to whom it is not related by blood, someone who is going to be more **OBJECTIVE**.

Of course, there have to be rules in pre-school, and lucky the child who experiences the enforcement of these rules in a nurturing, loving, consistent environment. Lucky the child for whom structure, form, and repetition will cloak the rules. The rules will be embedded in the routine way things are done. Daily and weekly activities will create the boundaries that will be so clear that gratuitous rules won't be necessary, and the child can move in the confines of the expected rhythms in the blissful confidence that security brings.[4] Come time for the parent-teacher conference, and either party can be nonplussed by descriptions from the other side. The greater the discrepancy in expectations, the greater the discrepancy in behavior at home, or at school.

Indulging a child is a mother's prerogative, in fact, a mother's defining characteristic. But if the home does not set up some basic expectations, the transition to first grade will be all the harder.

Scamp won't be going to first grade. Still, some elements of socialization are necessary. This is not one of Scamp's conspicuous realms of success. It's customary for dog owners with an off-leash dog to take the measure of an oncoming dog and decide whether they should leash their dog or not. When a dog owner is walking his dog toward me, I can usually tell whether my dog off the leash is causing nervousness. The two dogs, if they are both leashed, will often strain against the leash. Scamp likes to rush the other dog, which is highly uncivilized. I often have Scamp sit to let the other dog pass peacefully, all the while that I'm admonishing Scamp to "be good" and "no barking" while holding a treat in my hand. Distracted, he sits quietly. The other dog, exhibiting manners from good to none, walks by, and Scamp is let go. If both dogs are off the leash, they generally sniff each other and just move on. But Scamp will often growl, the hair on his ruff will get rough, he may bare his teeth . . . all in all he can be scary. I know it's all pretense, and most of the time so does the other dog. But the other dog's owner is offended. Thus I've come to anticipate all this by just keeping Scamp close when other dogs pass by.

In first grade, such adjustments are required by the group, and the teacher, like a circus juggler, must keep hoops, plates, balls, and juggling pins from collapsing.

Chapter Eight

Child Whisperers

When Scamp first arrived, I was anything but a dog whisperer. He was so uncontrollable that a sudden shout seemed the only way. It took a few months, but eventually I discovered that Scamp understood the gravity of my commands to be in inverse proportion to the decibel level of my voice. In those first days and weeks, however, when he didn't have any manners whatsoever, my only way to interrupt his obnoxious behavior was to shake a jar of pennies at him. He'd be so startled by the noise that he stopped what he was doing, such as, say, jumping up at me to show affection with his quick and sharp little puppy teeth. If the penny jar was not at hand, I yelled. It's what you do. Parents do it. Teachers do it. Children do it. Animals do it too, in all their various squawks, growls, barks, and screeches. A sudden, loud vocalization gets attention, as every infant knows. I'd shout, and for a minute I'd feel I was in control. The success was short-lived. A minute later Scamp would be at it again. It was crazy making, and made me almost as obnoxious as my puppy. Within the first week, I replaced the jar of pennies with a pocket full of treats.

Scamp grasped the If-Then principle with the speed of instinct. It was up to me to practice and be consistent, and not have too many expectations all at once. For reasons that remain obscure to me, the very first command he learned related to feeding time. I did not relish being run over by Scamp as I put his bowl on the ground. So very early on, something like the day after he arrived, I held the bowl he knew to contain FOOD, and if he charged forward when I put it down, I picked it up again. It was awful, really, having to be so insistent, when I knew the dog was hungry. But the alternative, having the hungry dog run at me and jump up to nose the bowl, was worse. It didn't take Scamp at all long to learn to wait when I put the bowl down.

After that came "Sit!" Perhaps because he'd learned to "Sit!" somewhere already, or perhaps because he's just a smart dog, he learned fast that if he jumped up to greet me with a nip, and I said "Sit!" and he sat, he could easily trigger a treat. I gave him plenty of opportunities to practice. He gave me plenty of opportunities to practice. Half his breakfast kibble was meted out to him one piece at a time, treat by treat. From the start, Scamp revealed himself to be a good-natured beast. He wasn't out to be ornery. He was just unschooled.

It took about four months for Scamp to be civilized. By the end of those four months we had reached a new normal; I was in charge and Scamp was eager to please. Instead of launching commands at him in a voice that could fell trees, I could simply speak to him conversationally. Perhaps because it was, after all, a one-way conversation – though not, of course, a one-way communication – I found whispered commands to be sufficient. Then I went from a whisper to a gesture. He still chewed what he could get his teeth into, but he was no longer wild on the end of his leash, no longer wild at all. He'd calmed down a lot, and so had I.

I watched plenty of dog training videos, but mostly I relied on my years of classroom experience. Though I'd learned about **firmness, fairness, and consistency** in the classroom, and that was exactly what my pooch needed, I still didn't take it as a compliment when friends, confessing that they'd had their doubts about how I'd manage the wild dog, followed up their, "I thought you took on more than you could handle," with, "but then, once a teacher, always a teacher."

Admittedly, the decades spent in the classroom helped me to succeed with the dog. But to temper the dog, I had to be not just a teacher, but the leader of the pack, the alpha dog. I didn't find that either admirable, or pleasant. He was cute, though, and the challenge of subduing the rascal without hurling him against the wall appealed to me, and so I persevered. More than once I lost my temper, and thanked my stars that he was so forgiving. I never beat him, but I yelled. Scamp was utterly trusting, which helped, because I had to try to live up to that trust. He never feared me. In his foster home days, he must have been treated with kindness. He didn't like to be touched about the head, and he completely refused to be led by his collar. Something probably happened there. Shouting merely puzzled him. If I really lost it, and was on the verge of attacking him, he cowered. It's a brilliant gesture, that cowering; it certainly brought me to my senses with alacrity.

But if children cower in the presence of a teacher, something is terribly wrong. And yet, the loud, brassy teacher voice is a ubiquitous professional hazard, especially in unseasoned teachers. When I was starting out, I was very loud. I raised my voice and thought nothing of it. The children would stare blankly, then some smart aleck would make a rude remark, everyone would laugh, and I would lose my temper. Ugh! I hate to think about it. In the meantime, experience in the classroom has trained me. These days, when I raise my voice, I do so as a tactical measure. I use a firm, low, directed voice. In fact, I use my "command the dog" tone of voice. It works. Still, more often than not, when something untoward is brewing, I get very quiet. If, in a class where nonsense is hatching, I speak very, very softly, the whole class is focused like light in a prism.

So it was with Scamp. At this stage, three-and-a-half years into our relationship, I don't even have to whisper. I can merely fold my arms and he recognizes that I mean business. "The look" that a teacher can cultivate in the classroom ought to have an ingredient that Scamp cannot quite appreciate: humor. There's a German proverb that states, "Mit ihm (oder ihr) kann man Pferde stehlen." The literal translation is: you can steal horses with him (or her). It means, I can trust you. When you give a rascally child "the look" in the classroom, the child ought to feel she can steal horses with you. A wink ought to be implicit in "the look" even though that look needs to be intense enough to bring a child to his or her senses. If that look is the prelude to more serious consequences, it maintains its value, otherwise it becomes deflated, and just another thing easily ignored.

Scamp has a habit I recognize from the classroom. He will take his time to obey a command. He will stretch, or yawn, or if we're outside, he'll be overcome by the need to pee. These physical requirements, he seems to know, trump my commands. Like it or not, teachers are constantly giving commands. The difference between addressing the children and addressing Scamp is that Scamp neither needs nor wants a "Please."

Scamp requires unambiguous directness. Not only must I project absolute authority, I must be so absolute in my expectation that my authority will be heeded. I must be firm and calm and undistracted by Scamp's distracting maneuvers.

Experience in the classroom with children has taught me that getting the children's attention is the way to achieve just about anything. I call it the "tennis court approach." Whatever Scamp's genetic progenitors, whether Vizsla, Kelpie, or any of a myriad Other, he is not a natural-born retriever. I wanted him to "Fetch!" so that he would get his exercise on days I couldn't, or didn't feel I could, walk him. So to train him to retrieve a ball took not only an incremental approach, but required focusing his attention, which, for him, is generally an olfactory activity. Not only did he have to bring the ball back to me, he also had to "Drop it!" Chasing the ball was second nature. He was hard-wired to chase whatever was moving away from him, especially if it was on the ground. Whether that was a Kelpie herding instinct or a Vizsla hunting instinct, he took off after the target. In the dog park, when the mysterious chemistry of dog friend was just right, he and the other dog would chase each other to the point of exhaustion. When it came to chasing a ball, he was reliable. Out on the wetlands trail I could count on having him get a good run, by sending the ball down the trail ahead of him. He'd pick it up, carry it a while, then drop it indifferently. Wherever we went, I watched jealously as other dog owners casually lobbed their "Chucky" balls into outer space, to have it returned by their panting dog. When I chucked the ball, I had to retrieve it. I tried the obvious: throw the ball not very far, and hold out a treat. Scamp followed the ball, then followed a wayward scent, abandoning my game. In my backyard, it was the same story. Then came the breakthrough idea.

In the nearby neighborhood park, there's a fenced tennis court. I took him in, closed both gates, and let him sniff to his heart's content, or better said, until his nose was content. Then I let him sniff the treat in my hand, rolled the ball about 10 feet toward the net and followed him as he followed the ball. He picked it up, and before he could abandon it, I took it from his mouth and (after making him "sit!") gave him his treat, one piece of ordinary kibble. From there it all progressed bit by bit, and before you could say Bob's Your Uncle, he was running to the other side of the court, and trotting back to me ball-in-mouth, then dropping it with an expert spin so that it rolled toward me. He got his exercise, and the tennis court surface served to keep his nails in check.

After a couple of months of tennis court retrievals, I tried hurling the ball toward the perimeter of the park, where a basketball court has a fence running along one side. We started with short distances, but now we're up to as far as I can chuck that ball. Conditions have to be right, though. If another dog appears, Scamp is as likely as not to forget about the ball. And just this morning I had to retrieve the ball a couple of times while he followed an undeniable scent. Also this morning, I tried chucking the ball the other way, into the park where there is no fence, just grass. Scamp is not ready for that yet. There are just too many interesting smells out there in the grass. So narrowing the field of attention is a strategy worth learning.

Generally, chaos in the classroom is the result of not having the children's attention. The children are already in a confined space, so the "tennis court" depends on the success of attention-getting devices that the teacher must invent.

Whatever the grown-up does, just remember that if you don't want the children to do it, you shouldn't do it either. Young children are great imitators. If you start to clap, they will too. If you start to sing, so will they. If you start to shout, there may be a sudden lull in their chatter, but soon they will shout too. No, shouting is not an option, much as you might feel like it. The thinner your reserves, the more the children will test your patience. They are masters of bad timing. You didn't get enough sleep last night? You have a headache? You're worried about your teenage son's drinking? Children have an unerring sense for what's up with you, and they are not merciful. It's not in their nature to be magnanimous. It's not in their nature to be forgiving. Mercy, magnanimity, forgiveness . . . these are attributes striving adults might seek. Children have to be raised to value them. Left to their own devices, they will merely exploit the weakness they sniff out in you.

So when you stand in a chaotic classroom, come up with something that is compelling. It might have a touch of mystery in it. One of my favorite stratagems is to go to the board and start drawing something. Perhaps it's a house, a simple house, with a four-stroke box supporting a triangular roof:

I draw it in white chalk. Then (if the children already know their numbers) I number the lines. (If they haven't yet learned the numbers, no matter, just skip the numbers.) By now most of the children are watching. Now I take a piece of colored chalk and then, very deliberately, use it to go over one line. If we haven't got quiet yet, we can add a second color for a second line. What the little house means is that the class has six warnings before there's a consequence. If you want fewer, start with a triangle alone, and so forth. In the older grades, even as far up as 7th grade, I sometimes resort to a design of dots, where connecting the dots would spell out a loud child's name. There's an element of drama and humor in all this, which the children appreciate. One of my first tricks as a novice 7th grade teacher was the "bank." The children owed me seconds, or I owed them seconds. If they took my time, they owed me seconds. If they gave me time, I owed them seconds. I merely had to start looking at my watch, perhaps with one hand holding a piece of chalk and poised to write under the debit column, for there to be silence. When Jamie objected that I was not accurate in my time keeping, I made him the time-keeper, and now we all knew we'd have reliable data.

So the "tennis court" approach means that conditions have to be created that make the exercise possible. In a classroom, if everyone is talking, you can't teach. In recent teaching stints, in 7th and 8th grades, I've used my Scamp lessons to be objective and absolute. I have only one rule: only one person talks at a time. If I'm talking, you're not.

If you're talking, I can listen to only one voice. Simple as it sounds, it's an endless drill, and requires endless repetition and utmost relentlessness.

In first grade, when the children are noisy (which in and of itself is not a bad thing, they just have a lot to talk about) and you cannot make yourself heard, do something. If the house on the blackboard is too subtle, do something more dramatic. Hold up both hands (or one hand) and start folding your fingers one at a time. The idea is that the children should be quiet by the time your hand is a fist. This can be practiced. Start it as a game. Start it as a drill. Perhaps the children stand as they watch your hand, and sit when the hand is a fist. There's always someone in the class who shushes the classmates, wants things to be just so, works as your apprentice. If your classroom is a place where fun things are being tried out, the children will soon be your collaborators.

One detail of infinite importance is that when once the magic silence manifests, it should not be stretched. You need to know what to do when the conditions you want are in place.

Whereas all I need to keep Scamp interested is a pocket full of kibble, what a teacher, especially a first grade teacher needs is a pocket full of tricks. By tricks I mean that the teacher needs to have a definite game plan. If the teaching moment is squandered, the children are less likely to cooperate in creating it the next time.

Scamp expects a treat every time he returns to me with the ball. If there is no reward, he may get the ball one more time, possibly even twice. But then the jig is up.

Children are forgiving, but don't disappoint them. Rewards, too, must be consistent, consequent, fair.

Fair means to be objective. As we saw in Chapter 7, objectivity is not always easy. To which I want to add: It is vastly easier to treat a dog like a dog and be objective than it is to treat a child like a human being and be objective.

Adult leadership is forever; inconsistency triggers confusion and anxiety in a dog and hyper dog behavior. Animal pack leaders never waver from their leadership role, and neither should you!

Ah, but there are times when we should waiver in our dealings with children. We are not just the alpha dog, who "doesn't negotiate to get what he or she wants." Only institutions apply rules indiscriminately. For the human caregiver of a human youngster, the true achievement comes from having the wisdom to know when the situation is exceptional.

Chapter Nine
No One Takes Me Seriously

Baby talk is the equivalent of teaching a child to ride a bike by providing ski boots as footwear. It's counterproductive. It's a handicap. It's cruel. Yet there seems to be something in the adorably complacent expression of an infant that incites cooing. I'm not referring to expressions of endearment, but rather to meaningless patter, to syllables without content. Whereas we would be hard-pressed to speak stupidly to a child who is already talking, we indulge in gobbledygook as we lean over the stroller. The little one has no way of knowing which part of the talk it hears is worth imitating.

Learning to talk is surely a superhuman achievement, second only to learning to walk. As a grown-up, you can glimpse the enormity of the effort required for either of these accomplishments if illness or accident has taken them from you. Why then would we want to put weights on a child coming to terms with gravity, or marbles in the mouth of a child mastering the extraordinary complexity of timing, breath and physiognomy required to speak? We wouldn't. Yet we babble incessantly. Silence scares us.

Getting Scamp to pay attention to his name, to listen to me when I spoke to him, was akin to getting a classroom of middle schoolers to interrupt their compelling chatter and look up. The very worst way to make progress in this regard is to talk without purpose.

I know nothing about how service dogs are trained, but I assume that one of the rules for the trainers is not to give unnecessary commands, not to teach unnecessary tricks. Scamp has learned only commands that I find useful for our life together. Did he flake out on the Roll Over! command because I thought it was a waste of time? Very likely. Sit! Stay! Drop it! on the other hand, are all eminently useful, not to say absolutely necessary. Equally practical are Leave it! Come! Fetch! Catch! Scamp has a habit of barking maniacally when a dog is walked past the house, especially if the dog is on the sidewalk on the other side of the back yard fence. Along the fence, where mulch makes for a warm bed on a sunny day, Scamp will snooze contentedly for hours. When a dog is being walked half a block away, however, Scamp's fur flies up, he prances and paws, and barks piercingly as the dog passes the fence. Why don't I train him to stop this nonsense, which shatters the peace of the neighborhood? Because the truth is I like having him be territorial. One of my initial motives for wanting a dog was that I wanted the protection of an early warning system. Scamp's bark is certainly a whole lot louder than his bite, especially when he's rigid with animosity and barking at full throttle. I have tried to curb the barking, by interrupting him with an unmistakable "No!" then bringing him in.

Over time, he's seems to be limiting the length of his rant. But I'll have to deal with my own ambivalence before making him shut up.

Growing up takes a couple of decades, and then continues, if we're lucky, for the rest of our lives. What a blessing for the growing human being if he is not asked to learn things unnecessarily, or only to satisfy some grown-up fancy.

Ideally we wouldn't be asking our charges to circle in place when what they really need is forward momentum.

Chapter Ten

Tight Ship, Tight Leash

A classroom run like a tight ship is desirable, a dog walked on a tight leash is not.

Tight Ship: A well-managed organization, as in, "The camp director runs a tight ship." This metaphoric term alludes to a ship in which the ropes are taut and by extension the ship is strictly managed.[5]

What could be more desirable than a well-managed classroom, most especially, a well-managed first grade classroom? Well-managed would imply that the sailors know their jobs and are scrubbing the decks with alacrity. When I walk into a first grade where there is a quiet buzz of activity, where the teacher is not immediately visible, perhaps because she is kneeling by one child's desk and all the other children are intent on their work, I call that a well-managed ship. It takes very little, though, for the sailors to be distracted, for the sails to hang limply, and the ship to veer off course. If little Joey jumps up out of sheer interest in his friend's progress with the task at hand, and that friend, Pat, happens to sit on the far side of the classroom, and Joey happens to pull Sally's pony tail as he passes her desk, and Sally yells, the attentive hum of engagement can quickly crescendo into shattering noise. A firm captain needs to anticipate the crew's penchant for distraction.

First graders are, by nature, frolicsome. The business of working at a desk is not innate. It must be learned. Many bothersome habits have to be achieved as prerequisites. The most obvious is just learning to stay seated. Plenty of times I've seen a child tilt a chair to the tipping point. Miraculously, I've never seen a child hurt by the maneuver. Although swiveling a chair on one leg allows a restless child to move more than sitting on a chair with four legs on the ground, it's not a good habit; both the furniture and the child's bones are at risk. So a class of frolicsome children for whom work at a desk is often utterly alien and bizarre, being desk-bound is as unnatural as being quiet and staying seated. It's a hurdle comparable to having Scamp knit. But whereas Scamp will never grasp a knitting needle, first graders can, and must, learn to sit quietly. An experienced hand on the tiller will realize that silence on board is not to be expected; it isn't a natural ability. Children blurt. They think out loud. Because being quiet is not a natural habit, Joey, who is particularly uninterested in the random shape of written letters, and much more interested in the lizards he and Pat have been finding in the stone wall during recess, will be endlessly creative in causing distraction such that he is relieved of the necessity of sitting at that desk, and he gets a good laugh from his classmates while he's at it. So when Joey casually strolls across the classroom toward Pat's desk, it's up to the teacher to decide instantaneously whether this is a moment to trim the jib or not. If it is, do we address only Joey, or do we address the class? Do we have to isolate this habit-detail, and practice raising our hand to ask to be permitted to get out of our seat?

There is one incontrovertible direction to this tightening process. You can always loosen your grip later. The reverse is not true. Once you have a tight ship, a "strictly managed" classroom, you can loosen the ropes or, to mix the metaphor, the reins. Once the children are in the habit of requesting permission to leave their seats, and their reasons will be legion – tissue, toilet, pencil sharpener, water, paper, sweater – and once you have proved a hundred times that you do have eyes in the back of your head and will not let a Joey-jump-up go unheeded, you can allow some slippage. Make sure, though, that you are playing the rope out very, very gradually, or it will spin out of control and the ship will list. It's a wonderful thing when the children, around third grade, begin to have the sense, on their own, about what is okay and what is not okay. But to expect such insights any earlier, without careful guidance, is to ask a blind sailor to navigate. We hold a toddler by the hand. We trust a teenager with our car keys. It's the long trajectory called parenting. *Education Toward Freedom* is more than a slogan; it's a practical goal. Freedom, in this case, means, the freedom to do what's right. Although ours is an increasingly "anything goes" culture, we still have the good sense not to send a toddler on the subway by himself. In many other instances, however, desperation presses us to bow to the child's will. We know that a child's will is steely, persistent, grating. The crying infant, the screaming toddler, the grumpy fourth grader, the sour adolescent, they test us. They want to know whether there's a captain to help steer them. Their own captain, their own grown-up self, is still in the making, and if fortune smiles, continues to be in the making throughout life. Fortune does not smile indiscriminately. Thus there are plenty of adults who have not grown-up.

In the classroom, a captain is indispensable. A captain can be strict without being harsh. Despite the Ahabs and Jack Sparrows, there are also the "Sirs"[6] and John Keatings. Numerous are the biographies that have been nudged by a discerning teacher. The discerning teacher, the grown-up who almost preternaturally recognizes what is not yet there, must be a good captain. A good captain in the classroom leads by force of example, leads by being "pedagogical." In the classroom, unlike on the ship, the captain is working invisibly and transparently. He leads through enthusiasm, not fear. Sending a child to walk the plank is not an option.

Scamp's third leash was a metal chain. He couldn't bite through it. Still, he pulled without restraint, and though he weighed only 27.8 pounds when I got him, it was hard on my hands and arms to keep him in check. In my less charitable and more exhausted moments, I wished I had a bit to put in his mouth. I considered a choke collar. Since he was choking himself when he strained against the leash, surely a choke collar wouldn't be much worse. Choke collars are also called training collars. Some look like instruments of torture, with sadistic spikes intended to hurt. No, it wasn't really an option. Then, luckily, friends suggested a harness. The leash was attached to the top of the harness, on the dog's back. Presto! Scamp walked by my side; he no longer rushed ahead in his impatient frenzy to investigate the next smell. Someone had designed a "pedagogical" device, a harness that enabled me and the dog to walk a-pace.

The average human being – child, teen, adult – can walk down the street and keep going in spite of possible distractions. We can admire the clouds and our legs can keep stepping; we can stop before crossing the road, without forgetting where we're going; we can even stop to sniff the roses, and then continue. Not so a dog.

> Dogs have 20 times more scent receptor cells than humans, and the scent-processing section of their brains is larger than ours. Where we might say, "Mmmmm, burgers!" a dog would say, "Mmmmm, fried ground cow muscle, gristle, and fat; soy extender; imitation American cheese made with vegetable oil and dry milk; wheat bun, toasted; a dozen sesame seeds; one leaf day-old lettuce; raw, partly green tomato slice; vinegar and spices in a tomato-based sauce, all touched by the hands of a human that I know and who will give me some if I make a big enough pest of myself!"[7]

The dog is built to smell. What ears are to a bat, or a tail is to a beaver, the nose is to a dog. It's the canine version of the hawk's talons, the cow's stomach. Some dogs are so specialized, with a sniffing apparatus so sophisticated that, by comparison, even the most prominent human schnoz is a pathetic organ of no consequence.

The structure of a dog's nose gives it a sense of smell that is thousands of times better than a human being's. A dog's nose has two hundred million nasal olfactory receptors. Each receptor detects and identifies the minute odor molecules that are constantly flying off different objects. Of all a dog's senses, its sense of smell is the most highly developed. Dogs have about 50 times more olfactory (smell) receptors than humans do. These receptors occur in special sniffing cells deep in a dog's snout and are what allow a dog to "out-smell" humans. Dogs can sense odors at concentrations nearly 100 million times lower than humans can. They can detect some odors in parts per trillion. A dog can detect a teaspoon of sugar in a million gallons of water, or two Olympic-sized pools worth, or catch a whiff of one rotten apple in two million barrels.[8]

Sniffing the bare sidewalk may seem crazy, but it yields a wealth of information to your dog, whether it's the scent of the poodle next door or a whiff of the bacon sandwich someone dropped last week. [...] "Generally" dogs have an olfactory sense approximately 100,000 to 1,000,000 times more acute than a human's. A Bloodhound, (The dog with the highest sense of smell) has a 10,000,000 to 100,000,000 higher ability than a human.[9]

Another way to comprehend the magnitude of the canine snout, is to compare it to the human eye. Most of us have a rather dull range of smell awareness. Think of the range of colors we can name, and how paltry the choice of smell descriptors, in spite of millions spent by Chanel, Max Factor, or Estée Lauder.

If you make the analogy to vision, what you and I can see at a third of a mile, a dog could see more than 3,000 miles away and still see as well.[10]

Okay, 'nough said. When I let Scamp off the leash, and he checks the perimeter of the dog park, or runs ahead along the side of the path sniffing and leaving his calling card and sniffing again, he's reading the newspaper, checking his messages, trolling the grape vine. It's his nature. He's built to smell the world.

Scamp is so ruled by his nose that not even a treat tempts him to interrupt his olfactory investigations. When he's nose-to-ground and riveted by something he's unearthing, he doesn't hear me call him. He's "busy."

A daydreaming child is also "busy." Children are busy when they're doing nothing. Doing nothing in the sand box, on the couch, at the table, in the bathtub . . .

Then the child "attends" school. Attention must now be focused regardless of the child's interest. More significantly, attention must be focused regardless of the child's staying power, which needs to be sharpened gradually, patiently, slowly, and inexorably.

In my days as an English teacher, I used to start my classes with recitation of poems. The higher the grade, the longer this warm-up. But no matter which grade level I was facing, I always stretched the class's concentration just a fraction beyond the comfort zone. It took a few years before my timing was reliable. I had to practice holding them beyond their natural inclinations, but not so long that I was asking the impossible, not so long that the exercise resulted in counter-productive restlessness, or ill-will. I used to "tune" the class during these warm-up recitation sessions, and, incidentally, the kids learned a lot of fine poetry. The trophy for concentrated recitation would have been won by an 8th grade who learned almost all of "The Rime of the Ancient Mariner" by Coleridge – all the way through Part IV! It took the better part of the year, and at their graduation, great was their astonishment when I recited for them my version: "There Was An Ancient Schoolteacher."

Reading the extent of the comfort zone is akin to reading the wind when you're sailing. Anticipation is all. And yet, you might need to allow for some choppy water and persist in steering your craft through. When Michael Tilson Thomas is poised on his podium, he can count on the attention of the San Francisco Symphony. Very likely, every member of that orchestra achieved membership because of above-average concentration as a child. When you practice an instrument, you have to keep at it. You have to go beyond the comfort zone or you'll never make progress. True, a teacher is a conductor, and sweet is the moment, often in second grade, when your orchestra is tuned and ready. Generally, though, the pupils' attention is wanting; they pay no attention to you, the teacher, unless you demand it.

In first grade we have to stretch the comfort zone, but not to the breaking point. Children with a "concentration problem" are children who find the task at hand unengaging. Often, the lack of interest is in direct proportion to a lack of understanding; the inverse can also happen: the child has powered through the task in half the allotted time, and now needs more to do. In first grade, progress in concentration, learning to do something longer than you would if left to your own devices, is the foundation of just about anything you'll ever learn. Why are the so-called "good" students often good at math? Because mathematics requires explicit focus and concentration, like chess.

Children can be taught to concentrate. School would be so much more fun if teachers didn't presume that concentration is something that happens on its own. It needs to be practiced. We have to help the children ignore the stray whiff. It takes maturity to stay focused when you're desk-mate is performing tricks. If you're the one performing the tricks, you obviously don't want to perform the teacher's tricks, and then the teacher needs to find out why. Different classes have different ranges for their comfort zones of concentration. And these zones are a bit like weather zones: shifty.

A whirlwind here, a glacial patch there, and all your best laid plans as a teacher will be ruined. Can you anticipate the weather? Can you teach the children to ignore the weather? Yes and yes.

I try to avoid calling Scamp in vain. If we're out on a trail, and he's running ahead, I try not to call him just to practice my sovereignty. It's tempting to call him, just for the satisfaction of seeing him run toward me. I try to avoid that temptation. I try not to fool myself into thinking I have a reason for calling him when the real reason is that it will boost my ego. When he does race toward me, I reward him with a treat. If I disappoint him more than once, he is a lot less eager to respond to my call. He will deliberately veer off the path, find something compelling, and ignore me. He's no fool.

Chapter Eleven

Treats and Punishments

The "treat" we humans should eventually respond to is the job well done. That's a bar so high and rarefied, that basic as it is, doing something for its own value entitles you to "saint", "artist", or "lunatic". Humanity seems to be intent on obscuring the very notion that a human's value is intrinsic. "Buy! "Work! Make money! Buy!" is the world-wide mantram. Yet, in spite of the massive allure, influence, and power of the "Start-up Entrepreneur" and all that is implied by those magical words, there continues to be a broad base of resistance to the notion that the only yardstick for success is accumulated wealth. Idealism is not yet dead. Hence, "Occupy Wall Street." As a movement it was short-lived. It didn't have the reach of flower power, but it dented the otherwise impenetrable gloss foisted on us by the controlling interests of banks, stock exchanges, and captains of commerce. According to those bastions of material success, there is no other goal but money. Having inflated our economy on the false promise of more and more and more money, they then burst the bubble and created the fiscal crisis we are still chronicling in our politics, talk shows, and films.

The Big Short was the flame feeding "The Bern." Yet the culprits remain as powerful as ever. Confronted by that kind of fortress, what's the little (wo)man-on-the-street to do?

Indisputably, every human being is an utterly negligible fraction of the world's 7.4 billion people. Mysteriously though, I am the only person in the universe who can say "I" and mean myself. Whether we identify ourselves as the former or the latter becomes a paramount marker in our destiny. Am I a meaningless cipher on the world's stage, or am I valuable because I'm unique? There's no question that the powerful billionaire puppeteers, the so-called 1%, expect the marginalized 99% to feel inferior and worthless unless the material values flaunted by that 1% are embraced. If you don't have a smart phone, you can't be all that smart, right?

What does it take to withstand the battering ram of commercials? Little wonder that "commercial" is another word for advertisement. The consumer upholds the economy by buying into the feeding frenzy stimulated by marketers. Marketers whip up our desires and subvert our discrimination. We are being driven by commerce and materialism to give up any shred of individual thinking. We are being flagellated by a ubiquitous and impenetrable scam intent on convincing us that *who we are* doesn't matter, and *what we have* matters a lot. That attitude is not our birthright. It is foisted upon us and by the time a child is a teenager, unless that family is off the grid, that teenager will surely have acquiesced to the system. The system, in fact, markets most fiendishly, to the impressionable, uncertain, herd instinct of the modern teenager.

We should take care, therefore, about the system of rewards we establish in the classroom. The reward for a child starting the long road called education will be immeasurably enriched if motivation is a teacher's smile, encouraging nod, praise, or appreciation. Perhaps a gold star is okay. Or an acorn. But when little children are rewarded with commercial success, or success that smacks of commercials, or encourages commerce, the child's childhood is sapped. The slope toward greed is sticky; soon the child will be in thrall to stuff.

"Good boy, Scamp" elicits a wagging tail and a nose nuzzling my hand, looking for that treat. When starting out with Scamp's training, I made the mistake of waiting too long to exchange the treat for verbal praise. At first, my voice impressed him not at all, no matter its pitch, timbre, or decibel level. I got used to controlling him with a treat, one piece of his ordinary kibble. By now he is alerted by my voice; he reads my body language and waits to be told what to do. His wagging tail expresses interest. Still, to get his full attention, I need to follow up with a treat.

We think we are motivating children to be good students when we grade them. We set up abstract categories, instigate an atmosphere of competition, force the child into someone else's template. It's a set-up that works well for the chameleon child, the child who can accommodate the template. It's a form of dressage and suits the ambitious child who quickly understands the values of the

1%, and doesn't mind conforming; it doesn't work well at all for the child who has her own sense of herself and her own individuality. And yet your own sense for just about everything is what you need when you grow up. It's your own sense of values that just might buck the illusion that you are nothing but a cipher, a cog, a replaceable part. Look at any self-help shelf and see how much of it is about self-validation, self-esteem, self-empowerment . . . Self!

Rewarding children individually, whether with a smile, an encouraging nod, a phrase of praise, or a written comment of appreciation; whether with a gold star, or a B+, challenges a teacher. It's a challenge because, as a teacher, you have to be honest. When these "rewards" come without cause, without having been honestly earned, a tragedy occurs. The child can no longer trust the teacher. Children are surprisingly unsentimental about their own efforts. They are realistic in their appraisal of others. Praise for a real effort is encouragement; praise for a desultory effort is dispiriting. The inherent complication in your average classroom is the range of abilities. A group of children often includes at least one whose best is another's worst. The art of teaching requires the insight to gauge when praise is legitimate. You have to know the children.

Conceiving a child, whatever the genealogy of the forbears, does not predetermine the result. You don't know exactly what you're getting. Even when there are genetic predispositions, the child is its own self. Finding that self is the task of any biography. There are false starts, aberrations, illusory successes. It's slow work.

By adolescence, the individuality has not only emerged, but is making every effort to distinguish itself. That individuation includes, but is not limited to, messing with the physique, the physiognomy, the color of the hair, patterns on the skin, clothing. It's that wide-spread adolescent desire for individual distinction that ironically leads to the herd mentality so successfully exploited by advertisers and social media. Social media rely on the youngsters' impossible yearning for individuation by cloning. Hide in the herd, and you won't have to prove your Self. Behind the growth spurts of adolescents hides a teen whose self is soft, not yet fully baked, shy, immature. It relies on camouflage by grouping.

Growth, physical growth, is of course one of the attributes of childhood. Under normal circumstances, children get bigger and taller without the help of the grown-ups who have gone before. It just happens. The other kind of growth, the inner growth that leads to maturity, which bridges the fraught gap between adolescence and adulthood, and to which we allude when we ask "Where are the grown-ups?" is a whole lot more subtle and complex in nature, and doesn't "just happen."

Having been an animal-obsessed child who often sought solace in their company, I should not have been surprised by the paragraph below that attributes something like inner comportment to the standards of obvious outer comportment as the goals of the dog breeder.

In addition to assessing physical characteristics, judges assess the dog's walk (gait) and attitude. For instance, criteria might require that the dog's attitude be cheerful, as for the beagle, or proud, as for the poodle. The American Kennel Club (AKC) has assembled these criteria for each of their recognized breeds. It gathers this information from the clubs and organizations that specialize in those breeds. The dog that the judges think matches its breed's criteria the best wins the competition.[11]

So a particular breed has a particular temperament. Decide on the breed and you'll be rewarded with a particular temperament. In the casual dog-owner chatter of the dog park, I often inquire as to the breed, and am usually met with a grin and a shrug and the explanation: "rescue dog." That's rescue as in a dog who's been rescued, not a rescue dog like a St. Bernard. It seems that many smitten dog owners accepted a pig in a poke, a dog in a cage, and are happy with their mongrel pet. Recently I became acquainted with a French Bulldog puppy. His owner explained that she had looked for a dog who did not need much exercise, would be happy on his own at home, and was small. Another neighborhood purebred I see regularly is the Cavalier King Charles Spaniel. But these nameable breeds are the exceptions. The mongrels from the shelter aren't free, but of course, without a pedigree, they're much less expensive, and perhaps that's a partial explanation. But I have wondered whether there's a relationship between the popularity of uncategorizable dogs, and the industrial effort toward homogenization of humans?

Scamp is a good-natured beast, and his natural "attitude" is cheerful. On a daily basis he surprises me with his expressions of joy. He can express happiness with such zest that chairs topple and rugs furl. He dashes about. He goes into high gear and I have to move fast to get him outside into the yard where he will race around for a couple of minutes to run off his excitement.

Usually these exhibitions occur when we have visitors. Scamp loves visitors and he reacts with high excitement when someone comes a-calling. Now that he's almost four-and-a-half, he has calmed down a lot about the visitors, but there are other reasons for expressing joy: when he sees me reach for my boot, or my coat, he exuberantly chases his tail to the point of swaying in woozy dizziness.

Do I want to prevent this show of Scamp's emotions? Certainly not. It's endearing to see my dog be so happy. A part of me doesn't want him to be a lackluster creature without interest in the world. The other part of me knows that to call it "happiness" is not quite right. Excitement? Yes. But happiness? One thing I'm pretty certain of: he doesn't really know that he's happy. He just is happIn any event, he's basically a well-disposed dog. He came that way. It's in the nature of his nameless unknown breed.

By the time children are in kindergarten, many of them have identifiable attributes: bossy, shy, aggressive, sly, cooperative, competitive . . . Unlike the purebred Cavalier King Charles Spaniel, however, which is "known for being affectionate, cheerful, courageous, gentle, and social,"[12] a child is infinitely more complex. What parent has not been astonished by his or her progeny. "I thought I knew my son, I thought I knew my daughter." These confessions are elicited by our unpredictable offspring, no matter their age. Predictability cloaks us ever more as we age. The predictability of our kith and kin, our colleagues, our politicians . . . it's enough to make us roll our eyes. Little Lucia, on the other hand, is still so malleable as to be unpredictable. Therein lie her parents hopes and fears.

One of the most successful young men I know, I'll call him Thomas, is the son of an obsessively active mother. I've seen the boy grow up, and it's a wonder to me that instead of being either swept into his mother's restless intensity or rejecting any hint of meaningful activity, he's developed into a calm, well-adjusted, strongly motivated but not excessively ambitious college student. Thomas certainly makes the case for Nurture, not Nature. Not all children are as self-directed. No dog is.

There's a website for Dog-and-Owner-Look-Alikes. I suspect that some of the images were doctored, but no matter. In the decades between dogs, I'd noticed it myself: dogs taking on the appearance of their masters. Look alike is one thing, but be alike is another. Dog neuroses most usually have their origins in the owner's neuroses. I don't consider myself all that well-disposed, and can't take credit for Scamp's outbursts of happiness. But I know I've calmed him down quite a bit, without beating the crap out of him. If the dog does something stupid, roll up that newspaper and beat yourself on the head with it. It's the scary truth. To calm my excitable pooch, I had to fathom my own reservoirs of calm. I didn't always manage. His formidable insistence on being the center of attention can make me bark even now. But on the whole it is a great help to realize that Patience with a capital P is all. You can't hurry the training of the dog, as the wise old shepherd on YouTube pointed out in Chapter Four.

Barrels of adult anxiety, nay, oceans of it, would be unnecessary if parents and teachers would just be in less of a hurry. Growing up takes time. Learning takes time. Some tricks are not feasible for everyone, and why should everyone learn the same tricks when everyone has their own?

Scamp can jump like a cat. He's learned to jump over a stick. I can raise the stick higher and higher. He needs no running start. The muscles in his thighs are strong. But Scamp doesn't really have it in him to be truly fierce. Protective, yes. Territorial, yes. But it's hard to imagine him grabbing someone by the arm with his teeth. Scamp, whatever his unknown ancestry, is a herder, a hunter, a pointer. I've seen him do all those things without anyone ever having taught him about them. What he is not, is fierce. Aggression is not part of his nature. He is a bit of an alpha posture, but definitely more bark than bite.

We don't expect a Rottweiler to be a circus dog. I don't expect Scamp to guard my bicycle. Here we find one of the undeniable distinctions between Scamp and any school child. Scamp's range of achievement is limited. In many ways, it is determined by his physique. Those pure bred show winners are all about physique. When we purchase a pure bred basset hound, we know what we're getting. I didn't know what I was getting with Scamp, but by now I know what I've got. I don't have a Rottweiler. I've individualized Scamp by domesticating him. He is a lot less complicated, a lot more generic than any child. Scamp never feels encouraged or dispirited. He lives only in the moment, and although the moment will have consequences, and a dog's spirit can be broken, he will never write his autobiography.

Human authors fabricate animal characters. Black Beauty, Lassie, and all the other animal stories I used to love, are, however, mostly anthropomorphized accounts. Perhaps the rampant popularity of the memoir is rooted in the atomized social structure we've cleverly barricaded ourselves into.

Sherry Turkle, author of *Reclaiming Conversation*, is a clinical psychologist and sociologist at MIT who has spent the past 30 years observing how people react and adapt to new technologies that change the way we communicate. She has also connected this research to the current loss of community in our information age. Turkle argues that texts, tweets, Facebook posts, emails, instant messages, and Snapchats—simultaneous, rapid-fire "sips" of online communication—have replaced face-to-face conversation, and that people are noticing the consequences. Over-reliance on devices, she argues, is harming our ability to have valuable face-to-face conversations, "the most human thing we do," by splitting our attention and diminishing our capacity for empathy.[13]

We teachers and parents, caregivers, uncles, grandmothers, and godparents, should take heed. Instead of being present (pun fully intended) only for birthdays and Christmas, let's be interested. Let's not rely on buying affection, on perpetrating the hoax of materialism, on rewarding with stuff. It's hard, but it can be done.

Chapter Twelve

Growling, Barking, Baring Teeth

Scamp once gave me a black eye. He jumped up as I bent down and his hard skull collided with my eyebrow. When I raised a tentative hand to my eye expecting blood, I found none, but by the next day I had a real shiner. Of course my friends all had that "I told you so" look on their faces, when during the following week they saw me with a swollen, purple cheekbone.

I've already mentioned his nippy ways when I first got him; how, during those long ago days, he nipped me to love me and loved to nip me.

Apart from that, he's been the epitome of gentleness. Nevertheless, there are situations in which he won't tolerate even me. If you touch him when he's eating, he growls menacingly. I'm quite respectful of that sound. I have, in a desultory manner, tried to wean him of this habit, but not very consistently. We have a truce of sorts: when I put his fresh water down beside him while he eats, he's not bothered. The key, though, is to know what irks him. Is it something I can live with, or must I cajole him into change?

Scamp grunts and growls when he plays, especially when he plays tug-o'-war, which he loves to do. I have to admit a certain wariness with that game, because one way he keeps his toothy grip is to snap at the rope close to my hand. In other games, he grunts with satisfaction when he snatches up a ball, or one of his favorite rag-toys. He's vocal. He has a keening whimper when, on our neighborhood walks, he smells or hears a dog behind a fence. It's a piteous sound, and I can't help but wonder whether he is sad about the prisoner, as he strolls outside the gate, albeit on a leash. In his limited way, he's got a range of expressive vocalizations. Compared to a snail, he's awesomely articulate. Compared to Ozzi, who is an eighteen-month old human, Scamp is mute. What they have in common, though, is the capacity, each in his own way, to tell you what they are feeling. When, in the back of my station wagon, Scamp emits his high-pitched hum, I start to look for a place where we can stop for relief. Ozzi is learning vocabulary by leaps and bounds. My friends Robert and Karen speak seven languages between them. Their daughter was brought up speaking four. A first grader, she is now learning a fifth. She is fluent in all of them, and doesn't get mixed up. Clearly, even for a human, this is a rarified achievement. It is also a truly human achievement. Scamp doesn't need to know whether he is speaking poodle or cocker spaniel. He has a universal canine language, and his tail, his fur, his ears are all part of it. The sounds he makes have their own nuance, and it behooves me to recognize the totality of his communication.

Children, too, often communicate without language. Their gait, posture, skin color, breathing, metabolism, nails can all talk to us. The younger the child, the less experienced the adult, the more mysterious is the story we're trying to read, the riddle we're trying to solve. "What you see is what you get," has become a maxim because it's so rare. Most of the time, especially as humans reach the age of puberty and beyond, the infinitely complex inner life of the human soul presents an ineffable landscape. My dog's inner life is primitively simple, by contrast. Nevertheless, his unrefined primary colors are instructive.

He can be fierce. When Scamp is in the house, and a dog is being walked along the sidewalk anywhere in sniffing range, Scamp breaks out in an ear-shattering, territorial volley. Sometimes I tempt fate by allowing him to patrol the front yard as I'm pruning roses or pulling at weeds. He used to run over to the neighbors to inspect their front yard and to see whether their miniature poodle, Lucky, was available for a game of chase. Now he mostly stays in the yard, wandering about, chewing on grass, sniffing the trails of last night's raccoons, rats, mice, quail, squirrel, skunks, and who knows what other visitors. Should a dog walker innocently come along the sidewalk, however, Scamp will charge. It's embarrassing. I have to apologize. The other night I took the garbage out and figured it was a good moment to let Scamp have his pre-bed pee, and just at that moment a young fellow and his nice little dog passed by and before I knew it Scamp had charged with a roar. The fellow pulled his dog back and the hair on both of them stood up with the shock of having Scamp hurtle at them with the power of a cannon ball. I gathered up my dog, muttered something about how he wouldn't hurt a flea, and retreated into the house where I should have rolled up a newspaper and hit myself on the head. Since then I haven't given in to the temptation to let him out unleashed into the front yard.

All these behaviors occur when the dog's territorial instincts are triggered. Only once did he have a tantrum without cause. At least, there was no cause that I could discern. Shortly after I got him, I was walking him back to the car from the dog park, when I saw that he had some goop in his eye. I reached into my pocket for a tissue. That's when he went crazy. He growled, he jumped, he pulled on the leash, he nipped me. I couldn't get him to calm down. He was frantically lunging in all directions, including straight at me. Providentially, there was a small stick by my feet. I let him clamp his jaws onto that, and with that to distract him, he placidly walked back to the car.

In the parks and on our walks, when he approaches another dog, the hair on his back stands up, his tail gets stiff, and he goes into a defensive growly mode. "Friendly?" I ask, indicating the other dog. If I get an affirmative answer, I quickly explain that my dog is friendly but growly. Most dog owners are not convinced. He looks menacing. I know it's all posturing. I'm as defensive as any mom when it comes to explaining my pet's bad habits. I think he was bullied by a dog during one of the times when I had to farm him out while I was away. To get him over his preemptive growliness, I have him sit, I conspicuously finger my treats pocket all the while telling him, "No barking, no growling." I've noticed that the oncoming owner is often muttering the same mantram. I keep Scamp distracted while the other canine passes by, and shower him with praise and give him a treat when he's managed to remain quietly seated during the encounter.

It doesn't always work. For reasons I cannot fathom, some dogs we encounter unpredictably cause him to lunge against the leash and bark like mad. And then there's James, a neighborhood character often on a skateboard, to whom Scamp is allergic. There's some antipathy there, and no matter how often we bump into James, Scamp has the same uncharacteristic response. Luckily, James is unfazed. If Scamp is off the leash when we run into James, the dog will run at him, barking up a storm, but keep his distance, while James stands there smiling.

Compared to the range of gratuitous negative behaviors in a child, Scamp doesn't have much of a range. The child's custom-made, individualized palette of fluid variations rightfully daunts us repeatedly, whereas I have my pet's moods pretty much figured. Yet, there are applicable overlaps.

In many, if not most, cases, the child will be sending a message similar to Scamp's. Almost always the message is a confusing combination of "Don't mess with me" and "Come play with me."

Children often growl preemptively. They are territorial. Their territory includes their toys. They have antipathies. And as with Scamp, distraction, avoidance, and not giving in to the (invariably selfish) temptation of allowing the child to engage in grown-up endeavors that stretch the child to the barking point, can ameliorate the growly tendencies.

One of the most distressing impressions a first grader can make on you is that she's really not ready to be in first grade. It's our adult ambition that forces that child into a school mode prematurely. Parental worries about the possibility of their child being slow in developing often create the very problems the worried parents are trying to avoid when they put the child in grade school too soon. Will the child "make it"? Let's make sure by giving him or her an early start. Of course, there are lots of practical reasons for getting the child out of the house, especially in the era of the working mom. So the child is taken to school. First it's pre-school. And many a behavioral caprice arises there. Often the cause is fear. The child has landed in alien territory where all sorts of inexplicable things are demanded. Who wouldn't be scared! The child is scared, and like Scamp, starts to growl. That growl takes on many shapes. A dog's growl is quickly identifiable. A child's is not. This is the realm of psychology, counseling, and therapy of every stripe. Like Scamp, though, the child both wants, and does not want, attention.

When I have guests, Scamp becomes an obnoxious creature. Knowing that he'll have no truck with me, he burrows into my well-mannered visitor, and becomes a pest. I suppose that if he weren't an "only child," or if he weren't the apple of my eye, or if he were a cat, he would be less of a jerk when he has to share me with someone else. His jealousy is insatiable. If I put him outside, he jumps up against the patio door, persistently. If I put him in another room, he scratches and whines, doggedly. Utterly exasperated, I put him in the back of my station wagon, which is neatly fit with a dog barrier. He jumps in eagerly because he associates it with a car ride no matter how often it's been his prison cell. I return to my living room with a feeble, "That's one thing you can't do with a child." It's feeble, because the dog should be trained out of his jealousy, his absolute need for attention. But it's another habit we haven't mastered. "He's only a dog," I say unconvincingly, trying to brush off the faint feeling of defeat.

"Time Out!" is the equivalent of the back of my station wagon. When all else fails, we isolate. We separate both dog and child from the environment in which its behavior is untenable. In the old days, standing in the corner wearing the dunce cap was considered remedial. Nowadays we try to avoid humiliation. The child is moved to a separate desk, is asked to stand by the back door, in the hallway, to go to the office. The attention-needer in the child is satisfied. But at what price?

In my experience, children don't "act out" without cause. Quite often the cause is positive. When a child blurts out the answer before the rest of the class has grasped the problem, the child is actually showing us his abilities. If Joey jumps up to see how Patrick is doing, Joey is following a social impulse. If Sally hits Devon because he took her blue pencil without asking for it, she's just being fair. Or is she? Deciding on an appropriate and effective consequence for undesirable behavior is often the hardest part of being a teacher.

Consequences, however, are essential. The guiding question ought to be: Does this consequence prevent the next example of similar behavior? But this is treacherous terrain. It might prevent undesirable behavior while quashing the individual who's behaving badly.

I never have to worry about Scamp's individuality. He doesn't really have one. He reflects mine. A child, from the get-go, has one. I just happen to have at hand Calvin Trillin's *Family Man*[14]. Trillin, journalist/humorist/food writer/poet/memoirist/novelist, captures human uniqueness in his inimitable way in a book he wrote when his two daughters were grown-ups.

> … our younger daughter, Sarah, had recently celebrated her first birthday, and I didn't think

of her as 'the one-year-old.' She was already extremely Sarah-like.[15]

Meaning, of course, that no child is like another. Yet in the classroom, children are expected to subjugate their personal predilections to the will of the teacher. Is any teacher ever really prepared for such responsibility? When the teacher asks the children to do what the children naturally want to do, then harmony reigns. The act of learning, however, frequently requires doing what is not (yet!) natural. You can't strengthen muscles weak in tone without pushing them beyond the comfort zone. So too with matters of comportment, as we saw in the previous chapter. Here is where the art of teaching comes in once again. Just as my friend, Adam, who's a wonderful chef, knows exactly how much cayenne to add to the Brussel sprouts, a master teacher needs to know the fine line between evoking interest, and creating chaos. The trouble is that one child's interest is another child's too much. Then that child, for whom it's all too much, will growl, and chaos alights. Now the teacher is presented with a mystery: why is it too much for Cedric when the rest of the class is contentedly practicing capital letters? And rather than punish the child, the teacher needs to set about solving the mystery. In the meantime, perhaps Cedric can be asked to clean the blackboard trays, or in some other way be temporarily relieved of his torment. If the torment is constitutional, a stomach ache, say, or poor eye sight, remedies are to be had. If the torment is in the home, it gets a lot trickier.

Because Scamp's life is not divided into school and home, I can't blame the teacher. I am the teacher. And I can't blame the parents, or the family, or the neighborhood. Quite often we resort to any of these to explain a child's proclivities, and there's every reason to recognize them as contributors to the child's unease. And the solution to the mystery of the child's individuality can also come by carefully studying the child. Can we find out what makes the child tick? There is a particular kind of first grade scamp that any teacher, as well as any puppy trainer, recognizes. This is a child, let's call him Raymond, who stares at you, takes the measure of you in an instant, has a robust appearance, and likes to tell everyone what to do. The mystery in this case is not concealed, but right there for all to see. Raymond is a born leader. Once you know this, he can become the first mate, under your command. Just remember to treat him with praise when he does the job well. As he leaves school, tell him that you'll call on him first during math drill, and that you'll be asking him to tell you the answer to how much is 4 times 7. The point is, play to his strengths, and support him. Don't try to obstruct him. Children are much stronger than the grown-ups whom life has already worn down.

Scamp is content to lie in the sun. At four-and-a-half years old, he's out of his puppyhood needs to be on the go most of the time. That's why, when he dances in circles in anticipation of our walk, or bothers me when I'm trying to read, he elicits a grin. Strength in children is something that ought to be preserved, and yet so much of our education aims to blunt their power.

I don't advocate the "open classroom," which some have extolled as the solution to variations in pace, ability, sociability, ambition, and the myriad of other factors that children carry into the classroom door. It doesn't really address the individuality of the children, and instead provides the illusion that they're profitably occupied. Left to his own devices, Scamp will eat garbage. Judgment is not something he can boast. First graders, in spite of their incredible powers of imitation, which can make them seem decisive, have none either.

So here's the rub: in first grade the individuality is latent. We've seen that first graders look a lot more like the people they'll become than they did as babies, and compared to twelfth graders, they are still babies. We treat them appropriately when we don't ask them to use muscles they don't yet have, muscles of judgment, abstraction, responsibility. We serve them well when we help them to persevere in the strengthening of capacities that require training to become useful. By the time they're eligible to drive, their own sense for what is right becomes a matter of life or death. Strengthening them without premature expectations means that we take the responsibility of providing our own judgment for them when they are little. When something isn't working, roll up a newspaper and hit yourself on the head.

Chapter Thirteen

Be Cool!

Some things benefit from desire. Your health, for example. Wanting to be healthy goes a long way toward a diet and lifestyle to support good health. Even when you're sick, wanting to be healthy can contribute to faster healing. Obviously, no one wants to be sick. So the "wanting to be healthy" I'm talking about is a really deep wanting. The kind that identifies with the thing wanted to such an extent that the wanter and the wanted merge. Being in love has the attributes of this sort of a wanting.

Being in love is a thing you can fall out of. Loving your own offspring should therefore not be about being in love. By growing up and becoming less cute, children manage to disengage from the overwhelming affection that parents are "programmed" to lavish. Postpartum depression has a name because it's an anomaly. Babies, whether cubs, fawns, lambs, kittens, puppies or human, are irresistible. Those for whom they are least resistible are the parents. In the animal kingdom, it takes anywhere from one day to five years for the animal to become independent. Among humans, the traditional age for "release" is 18, though there are instances of certain legal restrictions like having to be 21 to be able to smoke legally in California. Either way, a human parent continues to parent the child beyond the time of puberty. Unlike the baby she was, this adolescent is no longer necessarily cute, no longer cuddly, no longer dependent. And yet a human parent continues to be responsible for the child beyond the time when that offspring becomes sexually mature and seemingly rational – though this may be an oxymoron. These teenage years are inherently confusing for all. A large measure of confusion arises from the powerful, innate desire in a healthy adolescent to chuck parental influence. Parents, on the other hand, are still operating on habits of endearment. No longer in love with their progeny, they nonetheless continue to be carried by their desire to protect and support. It's a clash of desires.

All of which is to say that parents, by nature, are not cool toward their offspring. Flesh of my flesh is fused. Blood is thicker than water. Parents are not, nor should they be, cool toward their children.

Not so the teacher or trainer.

Whereas it would probably make a parent's job easier if he had a good dose of objective coolness to call on every once in a while, a teacher ought to rely on objectivity most of the time. A teacher in love with the children is headed for shipwreck. You simply can't get the little rascals to reach for higher standards than the wild proclivities they naturally harbor if you identify with them. As a teacher, you need to identify with what they are not yet.

Over the decades, I've seen a good many babies grow up, marry, and have their own children. It's enabled me to play a game I call, "Let's Imagine This Child Five, Ten, Twenty Years From Now." I've now reached the age myself where I no longer go beyond the Five and Ten, because this game can only be evaluated in the future.

The hit movie, *Boyhood*, also plays this game. I find it fascinating that the movie's appeal is that it does NOT imagine how the characters will look in the future, does not depend on make-up artists to age the faces of the cast. The director had the novel idea of following the actors through the years in real-time and allowing the audience to watch the real human beings actually age. Certainly that's a case of art imitating life if ever there was one. How very strange, I think, that prizes and plaudits are being showered on this movie. Its plot is pretty generic. It's a sort of Everyman story. What sets it apart is that it was filmed over the course of twelve years. Real life years. The characters in the film, which these actors represent, would be far less interesting if the ploy of showing the actual passing of time, by filming over the course of twelve years, weren't part of it.

So no imagination had to be applied to the physical metamorphosis the characters underwent during the twelve years. And THAT failure of imagination is being praised extravagantly. The movie won the Golden Globe Award for best motion picture in the Drama category. David Edelstein, the movie critic for the award winning NPR show, "Fresh Air," laid on his trowel of praise by defining the cumulative power of the movie as being "tremendous".

> Boyhood isn't a documentary but it has a documentary hook. Richard Linklater filmed actor Ellar Coltrane in intervals over 12 years. Beginning when Coltrane's character Mason was six, ending on the far side of puberty. We see the actor go from cute and compact to slightly pudgy, too long-waisted and handsome. We're used to time in cinema being relative, easily manipulated. But time actually passing is central to how we experience "Boyhood." We scan Coltrane's face and body for changes. We come to think of each moment as fleeting, irrecoverable and so precious.[16]

Gee, that's what I've been doing for ages with my game, "Let's Imagine This Child Five, Ten, Twenty Years From Now." The movie followed a script. The aging actors learned it. The movie's characters aged stereotypically, whereas the actors themselves probably did not.

Child actors have dismal lives on the whole, Shirley Temple being the oft-cited exception, because when they grow up, they go not only from "cute and compact to slightly pudgy and long-waisted" to quote Edelstein, but in time they thicken, shrink, sport wrinkles, grow bald. As commodities, they lose their appeal.

Parents are not supposed to find even their wrinkled, middle-aged children less appealing than the smooth skinned infants their babies once were. Teachers, on the other hand, ought never to fall for the appeal of even their cutest students. For teachers, appeal should never enter the equation. For teachers, the long view is absolutely desirable. That long view requires a strong measure of objectivity, so that the child is never absorbed into the teacher's personal domain. The parent's relationship to the child is, by definition, personal and subjective, meaning, the child is permanently part of the parent's identity. The teacher ought never to lean on the children for personal satisfaction. That's professionalism. Of course a teacher can be proud of the children's accomplishments. But that pride has to be the pride of the professional who recognizes the child's achievement and is proud on behalf of the child. A parent's pride is almost always personal. The parents feel the child's accomplishment reflects on herself.

A first grade teacher ought to have the power of imagination to have a sense for what's ahead. That's not to say that the teacher need be a prophet. The child, after all, is as likely to surprise us as not. But in my times of playing "Let's Imagine This Child Five, Ten, Twenty Years From Now," I've developed the means to see ahead in a way that the parent cannot. Generally speaking, parents are so enmeshed in the day-to-day logistics of child-rearing, that there simply isn't the time or the energy to look beyond tomorrow. Here's Calvin Trillin again:

"I always had trouble envisioning our children at any age other than the age they were right at the time."[17]

That about sums it up. I've noticed that even when there are older siblings who've metamorphosed into becoming themselves, the changes in the youngest take parents by surprise. As Trillin makes clear, it's hard for a parent to play "Let's Imagine This Child Five, Ten, Twenty Years From Now." But even if they had the time and the inclination to do so, they'd be unlikely to see their grown-up child as different either from what they expected the child to become, or from what the child once was. How many novels deal with just that? The so-called *Bildungsroman* details the struggle.

To be categorized in the genre Bildungsroman, the plot must follow a certain course. The protagonist grows from child to adult in the novel. An example of this genre could be the book *Johnny Tremain,* or *Tom Sawyer* or *Jane Eyre,* or *Little Women*[18]. At an early stage, a loss or some sort of discontent pushes him or her away from home or the family setting, providing an impetus to embark on a journey. The main character often develops through "self actualization." The process of maturation is long, strenuous and gradual, involving repeated clashes between the protagonist's needs and desires and the views and judgments enforced by an unbending social order.[19] It's the "push away from home or the family setting" I'm trying to get at.

A less formal description clarifies in even simpler terms:

A Bildungsroman is a story of education. It is similar to coming of age stories; however, the characteristics of the Bildungsroman are more specific. In order for a novel to be considered a true Bildungsroman, the main character has to experience some form of moral development. In essence, they have to grow up. The focus of the character's growth is the main thrust of the narrative.[20]

"In essence, they have to grow up." That's the nub of it, the heart of the matter. They leave home, they have adventures, they grow up. If economic necessities require that they do stay home, it's unlikely that they take over the restaurant business, or join Dad as a partner in construction. Or if they do, then only after the 'self-actualization,' which is 'long, strenuous and gradual.'

The popular Goodreads website[21] lists 2,944 *Bildungsroman* titles, starting with *The Catcher in the Rye* by J.D. Salinger, and ending with *Remembrance of Things Past: Volume III - The Captive, The Fugitive, & Time Regained* by Marcel Proust.

No doubt a PhD thesis exists somewhere detailing just how many *Bildungsroman* protagonists had to overcome parental expectations; no doubt this same PhD categorizes the incidents of rebellion along the lines of: hostile, violent, criminal, negligible, successful, unsuccessful, humorous, tragic, et cetera.

Literature has recognized this real-life theme as compelling. Parents, unlike authors, are less free to perceive this essential process of "development" and "growth." Although that process begins when the child is born, it is essentially invisible until the child starts to talk. You can't really perceive the independent "development" and "growth" of something that's as much a part of you as a newborn. That's why it's harder for mothers. For nine months mother and child shared a body, and it can easily take 21 years for detachment to be attained.

Scamp's "self-actualization" has also involved education. It even involves repeated clashes between the protagonist's needs and desires and the views and judgments enforced by an unbending social order.

It's a matter of Scamp as protagonist clashing with the judgment enforced by the unbending order of me, his master. To be Scamp's master, I need to be cool. Being cool with regard to Scamp is not a given. I love my mutt. But he is not flesh of my flesh, and water is thinner than blood, and the progress he makes is in direct proportion to my coolness, my distance. I cannot meld with the dog the way a parent is naturally disposed to meld with their progeny. I cannot, and I should not. Dog school enlightens the owner as much as it trains the pet. You cannot request a dog to obey. You need the attitude of a drill sergeant. Anything less will sound unconvincing.

Parents are well-advised to avoid sounding like drill sergeants. Perhaps in rare instances, they might resort to that tactic. Dog owners must habitually have the attitude of drill-sergeants, meaning they expect obedience, though they can, in time, learn to whisper their commands. Teachers fall into a large middle area.

A first grade teacher falls somewhere in the middle range on the spectrum between parental warmth and dog-trainer cool, between the parent's inborn subjectivity, and the dog-trainer's acquired objectivity. As the children grow older, teachers need to edge toward the cool pole. Yet even in first grade, school is school because the teacher is not Mom or Dad. Any child growing up in a supportive home knows that Mom and Dad (though probably Mom more than Dad due to the aforementioned body-sharing intimacy of those first nine months), are push-overs. Offspring know how to rule the roost. They are masters of timing. They are brilliant dramatists. They are geniuses of button-pushing. When they get to school, and especially to first grade, they have to discover that teachers are immune to their stratagems. Usually this period of adjustment is harder for the parents than for the children. Children are extraordinarily loose-jointed; conservative, yes, but resilient. They readily realize that school is not home, and that patterns of behavior that provoked victory on the home front, will cause barely a ripple at school. The Teacher should just be less impressed by little Terry's terrors. To be less impressed, Teacher must be cool. If Teacher goes up in smoke every time Terry throws a fit, it will only feed Terry's resolve to throw another. If Terry discovers that a fit is not needed to get Teacher's attention, Terry is less likely to resort to a fit.

Scamp has provoked me into more than one fit. The prime fit-provoking scenario involves lack of time, hence lack of patience on my part. If he's out in the yard, and I'm late for an appointment, and he practices deafness, I could, and often did, scream. That was before I became a dog-whisperer. My screaming naturally produced the very opposite of the desired effect. Instead of coming toward me, as I was insisting loudly he must RIGHT NOW DO YOU HEAR ME, he became even more interested in finding the perfect blade of grass – for whatever purpose. Looking back on those days, I can now see that I was the one fit to be tied. He was simply being his mild-mannered self, going about his business.

When grown-ups are over-invested in children's behavior, we have the beginnings of a *Bildungsroman*. When authors are over-invested in their dog protagonists, they have less to worry about. *Lassie* is probably the most famous of *Hundbildungsroman*, to coin a phrase, with *Call of the Wild*, *Big Red*, and *Old Yeller*[22] not far behind in popularity over time. *Hundbildungsroman* means dogbildungsroman, and is therefore an oxymoron. Dogs, despite their owners' contentions to the contrary, never know that they are going through that process of "self-actualization." The "self" of a dog is, as we've already noted, genetically determined. The dog can suffer, and all these classic dog tales show us how harsh their suffering can be, but they are not *aware* of their suffering with the consciousness humans bring to bear on their own condition. A sick dog, like a sick baby, is heart-rending because neither is self-actualized enough to tell you what's going on. They just have to bear it. You just have to do the best and then watch the suffering. Dementia and developmental delays; mental, emotional and physical breakdowns, these too cause so much torment in the beholder because the sufferer is dumb, mute[23].

It should be easier for the dog trainer to implement a regime of cool responses, because as a dog trainer you ought not to be emotionally invested in the outcome. As a parent you are, by definition, invested in the child's development, and it's a parental function to love the child unconditionally. When the child acts like a child, it's up to the parent to act like a grown-up. That's a mighty challenge, and uniquely so. How could we ever be invested in anything as much as in a being we've conceived? People talk about "my babies" referring to their backyard vegetables, or to the books they've written. Nonsense! No comparison. The act of artistic creation is still a paltry thing compared to the creation of a child.

Teachers, to be effective, meaning, to lead the child into its own future, must retain some cool. Emotional involvement in whether the child has learned to read is counter-productive. The child is not learning to read to provide you with a feather in your cap. Parents, teachers, and dog trainers will all achieve their desired results with less frustration if they are really, really detached from any outcomes. Children and canines can sniff out the least bit of ambition in their keepers, and in keeping to their natures, will instinctively thwart it. The trajectory from 1st to 12th grade is all about the need to find one's own ambitions, to determine and train one's own talents.

Scamp's only ambition is to feed his stomach. He knows no bounds. It's not in his nature to Sit! Stay! or Get Out of the Kitchen! He understands these things, and obeys, if I am as cool as a cucumber.

Terry, too, would be relieved if we were less likely to care about Terry's behavior. Inwardly, we care a lot. Outwardly, we have to be cool as a cucumber.

Chapter Fourteen
Food

We all have to eat. Deprived of nourishment, we starve. As grown-ups, we are meant to regulate our need for food. Was obesity a problem before the food industry spread its toxic tendrils into every morsel, changing nourishment into entertainment, catering to our unhealthiest cravings? "Food industry" is a contradiction in terms, but that hasn't stopped it from flourishing. It has even spawned its own anti-body, the diet industry. As if the giant maw of agribusiness with its gentech offspring and food factory excess weren't enough, our relationship to seasonal foods and the rhythm of meals has been pretty well destroyed by the blessings of electric light and refrigeration.

In the face of the impenetrable confusion engineered by product marketing, what's a new parent to do? A newborn's consumption of nourishment is a gigantic worry. There lies the helpless little drooling, peeing, pooping baby, and somehow the grown-ups have to regulate intake and outflow. Mom and Dad magically need to know what, when and how. Suckle-digest-expel-sleep-suckle-sleep-digest-expel. That's the life of a new born, and without it there can't be life in a newborn. It's a mighty process and the caregiver grown-ups are rightly obsessed with getting it right. There are endless theories about how to manage these vital components, including the self-serving suggestions from the baby-food investors.

As consumers grow increasingly removed from food production, the role of product creation, advertising, and publicity become the primary vehicles for information about food. With processed food as the dominant category, marketers have almost infinite possibilities in product creation.[24]

Food is product, product is processed, processed product is packaged, packaged processed food becomes the norm even for the newest, tiniest, most helpless infant. What's a sleep-deprived, well-meaning, suggestible parent to do? As soon as the baby is weaned, unnatural food stuffs insinuate themselves into the life of the infant. By the time the child can hold a spoon, it has discovered just how important for Mom and Dad the spoon's arc is. It doesn't take long before the child has learned that it can rule the roost with its eating habits, or lack thereof. Little children have a way of wrinkling their noses at the very foods we think will do them the most good. It's not that broccoli has an inherently bad taste, it's that we endow that green vegetable with super powers, and the child, picking up on our ambitions, pooh-poohs them. Children have an innate sense for foods they need. Many children avoid meat until they are ready for it; or don't want fruit; or dislike eggs, but this natural inclination is easily corrupted. Sugar, salt, fat . . . the usual suspects, are artfully smuggled into baby foods. So much has been written about food and its social, psychological, spiritual, and physical ramifications, that more is not needed here. My point is that food becomes one of the child's early control agents, and the hapless grown-up acquiesces, thus accomplishing the very opposite of what that grown-up wants more than anything, which is to do right by the child.

Refusing to eat broccoli, or turning away from yogurt, has never been detrimental to any child I've known, and I've seen plenty of picky eaters. Yet parents are often reduced to frustrated misery by a child's selectivity at the dinner table. No amount of reasoning or cajoling seems to help. What to do? I cannot offer a magic bullet, but when the parent becomes less invested in the child's diet, when the parent can be matter-of-fact about the food on the table, and have more of a take-it-or-leave-it attitude, wonders can be worked. It's difficult though, because as adults we feel responsible, and we feel desperate. We don't want the child to suffer the consequences of an inadequate diet. We don't want to put the child off its feed. In the tricky adolescent years, bulimia and anorexia haunt the dining room. No wonder that the signature phrase of the Jewish Mother is "Eat, my child, eat. How else will you become strong?" We worry about allergies, skin eruptions, lassitude, bowel movements, irritability. We worry about whether the child will still love us when every meal becomes a battle.

As I said at the outset, Scamp is voracious. He is always hungry. He will eat anything anywhere anytime. And I mean anything. He's not at all particular about the condition of food. Not that he minds quality. I cannot let him loose at the beach because he will happily eat the sandwich out of your hand even if your picnic blanket is in the dunes or along the cliff. He will run away from me at top speed and launch himself onto your blanket with a spray of sand and then snatch your chicken salad sandwich before you've blinked. Even when on the leash and on the sidewalk, he is quick and devious about grabbing windfall plums or rotting apples. Should you have dog treats in your pocket when we get to the park, he is likely to jump up at you.

I measure his food. When I first got him, my habitual question for fellow dog owners at the dog park was, "How much do you feed your dog?" People thought I was telling them their pooch was too skinny or too fat, but I was just looking for facts. My instinct was to give him too much. Eventually, by dint of research, conversation and just observing my pet's muscles, energy, and fur, I figured out what Scamp needed. He didn't need as much as I thought he did, and as he grew out of full puppyhood, he needed even less. So I measure his food, and don't allow myself to be generous with the measurement. I measure out the treats I think he'll need for the day – they're just his regular kibble – and he gets his rewards when we play or do tricks. I am rigorous about no scraps at the table. When there's a guest at the dinner table, Scamp tries to take advantage of the visitor's ignorance of the house rules. "Go away!" is one of the commands that Scamp understands perfectly well, but he knows that the guest is less likely to insist on it. When we're alone, I don't let Scamp near the table where I'm eating. When I feed him, I make Scamp wait outside the kitchen until I've filled his bowl and if he comes before he's called, I pick up his bowl and he has to go back and wait until he's called. It sounds easy enough, but it takes a relentlessness that can be exhausting. Clearly, what Scamp eats is not the issue, though I confess that I make a ground turkey supplement and add a three-oil combo to his morning meal. For all his gobbling, bolting, scarfing inclinations, his digestion is tender, and he's happiest when there are no variations to his routine. When I give in to his entreaties with pieces of carrot or apple, both Scamp and I have to deal with the messy aftermath.

If feeding dogs were as formulaic as feeding cattle or industrial chickens, there might not be as many overweight dogs. A pet's begging eyes are hard to resist. It takes a cool-headed, steely determination to resist. It takes a relentless adherence to the rules. It takes supreme trust in the power of your own convictions.

As we've already seen, a cool head is not a parent's natural mode. Even less easily accessible for parent or caregiver is reliance on the power of convictions. Those convictions have to be deeply rooted not to sway with the offspring's forcefulness. With all the theories swirling about, how is a parent to know what to do? Honestly, I don't know. Here's what I do know: the less the parent is invested in the child's eating habits, the more the parent leans toward the cool pole, the pole that exudes disinterest, the less the child will feel impelled to fire up the parent with obstinate eating. It goes without saying that the parent is not really disinterested, that the parent needs to keep a close watch on the child's diet and how that diet affects the child, but the child ought to feel free instead of coerced, pressed, or threatened about eating. The child is free to the extent that the parent is outwardly standoffish about the whole rigmarole, even when inwardly on tenterhooks.

Neither dogs nor children deal well with vagaries. What they crave is consistency. If we give in to their stratagems, they lose confidence in us. Given the least bit of parental insecurity, the child is quick to make food a currency of choice.

For grown-ups engaged with children, a habit of seeming indifference can be usefully cultivated. By seeming indifference I mean feigned indifference, not neglect. Moreover, this feigned indifference has to be sincere. That's a triple contradiction. We have to pretend not to care. We have to be actors.

Teachers, too, must hone their acting skills. Teachers cannot allow their personal lives to broach the classroom walls. If they are too sad or depressed to work, they really should stay home. The danger for teachers is that they forget that their act is not meant to elicit applause. It is meant to allow the child in the classroom to do what's right in freedom – eventually. Eventually, perhaps by 11th grade, a youngster can perform without performing for anyone but her or himself. It's ironic, because high school is the very age when kids have crushes on teachers, are inspired by teachers, need teachers to keep them on the straight and narrow. All true. But if the teacher finds satisfaction in the teenager's adulation, then we have a professional kink that, in the worst-case scenario, will lead to tragedy.

In early childhood and preschool, cuddles and hugs are a normal exchange. But woe to the teacher who becomes addicted to them. Even in primary school, all the way through 4th grade, the child's looking up to the teacher can act as a teacher-tonic. But that's unhealthy. Professionalism in a teacher is not a given when the client is cute, endearing, needy, impressionable. Imagine if your dentist's emotional life depended on you.

Once when I was recuperating at a clinic, I was in love with one of the doctors. Luckily, being older and wiser, he understood that what I was really in love with was the idea of getting healthier. Children do and ought to love their teachers. But teachers cannot depend on that love for emotional satisfaction. The whole point of education is to enable the child to find his or her own Self, not the overlay of what teachers have overlaid. Parents, on the other hand, are supposed to get emotional satisfaction from their children. Hence the bond. Hence the endless complications. Children are and should be parent-tonic. It's the prerogative of the parent to love the child, and feel the surge of warmth and primal identification that comes with that love. For the teacher, something less personal must be achieved.

When this distinction between home and school is on track, the child will often behave differently at home and at school. Ideally, when the child's impact on the environment is not as immediate at school as it is at home, there is less motivation for attracting attention. Children are geniuses in knowing how to push their parent's buttons. In an ideal world, teachers wouldn't have any buttons to push, nor would they have any chips on their shoulders. In the real world, teachers are well-advised to be free of the children, so that the children can be free of the teachers. Parents are never free of their children, and vice versa. This lack of mutual freedom has filled endless tomes of fiction and psychology. It is the ever-present and riveting drama of successive generations, and the stuff of every manner of media entertainment.

Not long ago I was separated from Scamp for a few months, and the way I missed the dog was embarrassing. Luckily, no one but I knew about it. Nor did my missing him interfere with my mood in any way. It was the habit of the creature being nearby that I missed. I missed the cat too, although cats being less dependent by nature, I was less dependent on feline attention, thus less aware of the cat's absence. A dog is just a dog. A cat is just a cat. A child is not just a child.

When a child discovers that food is one of the easiest ways to dominate a parent (or in extreme cases, the world), it's the parent who needs to roll up a newspaper and hit himself or herself on the head.

Chapter Fifteen

Anticipation

The reason that everyone talks about the weather is that no one can do anything about it, as Mark Twain famously pointed out. Weather is unpredictable. Oh, sure, meteorology is a world-wide weather prediction science, but the vagaries of local temperatures and precipitation totals elude even the sophistication of weather satellites and earnest meteorologists.

Here are excerpts from one version of a recent inexact prediction, as reported on the Internet:

> Meteorology and governing are inexact sciences. You have limited information to work with, tremendous time constraints, and way too many variables. You do the best with what you have and hope you get it right.

> With meteorologists predicting blizzard conditions and perhaps as much as 18 inches of snow for New York City, city and state officials moved quickly to shut down as much of the transportation system as possible. Highways were closed to all but essential personnel. The Metro-North and Long Island commuter railroads were shut down, and all bus and subway service was suspended at 11 pm Monday night.

When Tuesday came, the much-hyped storm was a bust, with New Yorkers standing in less than a foot of snow left wondering why the normally 24-hour subway—even the underground lines—had been shut down.

The story then pointed out that this inaccurate prediction wreaked financial havoc:

Effectively forcing millions of people to stay at home has obvious consequences: Shops and restaurants don't get business, public transit and taxis lose out on fares. People can't get to the pharmacy to pick up medicine, check on relatives, or get to the doctor's office. It's way harder for essential city employees to get to and from work.[25]

Predicting Scamp's vagaries is easier, getting them wrong less costly, and developing a forecast for his behavior is beneficially stress-reducing.

Out on our marshland levee walk, as we approach one of the ramps leading to a local street, I am on high alert as we pass the turn off to Al and Betty's place. Scamp knows there's a rich compost pile in that front yard. Being a creature totally managed by his stomach, he will contrive to get ahead of me on the path and then bound off toward that source of decomposing delights. The obvious deterrent is anticipation. If our walk is taking place before the dog was fed, or if he seems more self-determined than usual, I snap the leash to his harness well before we approach that ramp. There probably are dogs who can be trained to ignore olfactory input. Scamp is not one of them. Now that he's about four-and-a-half years old, he's not as rascally as he used to be, but still, when he's on the leash, he will thoughtlessly jerk me to a dead stop if he wants to smell the roses. Or the bushes. Or the grass. So in our neighborhood where traffic is scarce, I'll walk him in the middle of the road or on the street side of the sidewalk, just to keep my shoulder from being jerked out of its socket. He's learning that when we are walking on-leash, he cannot respond to all prior dog messages by stopping to lift his leg. "Obnoxious," is how one of his caretakers described this habit, which, I hadn't realized until she said it, it was. It really hadn't occurred to me that he didn't HAVE to do that. So now I anticipate his penchant for marking the hydrants and lamp poles and dog-telegraph vegetation, and tighten the leash and quicken my step and don't let him stop me. He is getting the picture.

In the heyday of my career as a teacher of children, I practiced the equivalent of testing the wind with a raised index finger by halting at the threshold of a classroom I was entering, to take the measure of the classroom weather. Was the din greater than usual? Was the outgoing teacher in a frenzy? Were children cradling their heads on their desks because they'd had an exhausting morning? I got good at "reading" the atmosphere. Then, after a few more years of practice, I got good at adjusting the lesson to meet local conditions. If the barometer in the room was rising because I was racing, I needed to adjust my pace, lessen my expectations for what could be accomplished in those 50 minutes. Was a dust devil waiting to explode in the back row because Kirk and Sue were teasing each other into an atmospheric disturbance? Then it would be prudent to keep them both occupied, each according to ability.

Some things could be habitually predicted. Monday mornings were likely to be chaotic as children settled back into school routines. Friday afternoons were likely to be stormy as children and teachers strained at the end of their tethers while the clock crawled toward the liberating bell. No matter that the children and the teacher were having a great time rehearsing a class play, or, in anticipation of the weekend's lure, avoiding stress by playing dodge ball in the school yard. Straining toward liberation was not contingent on any feeling of imprisonment. It was just a force, a sort of gulf stream of expectation.

When the routines and rhythms are reliable and healthy, so that children can do what needs to be done without being told, then unexpected incidents, the inevitable earthquakes and volcanic eruptions, can be met so much more easily. In chapters 3 and 4 we considered how to achieve some measure of routine. It's a long haul with endless repetitions.

This morning Scamp actually anticipated the need to sit down before I opened the door. Probably my body language alerted him, but still, I was pleased, inanely thinking it was my good work I was witnessing.

If we sustain the endless practice needed to establish good habits as routine, we can eliminate a lot of the terror that unexpected incidents precipitate. If the basic expectation is tranquility, it takes longer before agitation blossoms into a vortex. This is true of children at any age, at school and at home.

Let's say we're in the first grade, and all the children are working hard and silently to copy some words off the blackboard, and the teacher is walking from one desk to another, quietly commenting on this and that, and then little Annelise emits a loud gaseous evacuation; or Elroy accidentally (well, probably it was accidental) dumps all his colored pencils on the floor. If the fundamental expectation in that room is a placid mood, neither Annelise or Elroy will cause an inundating tsunami of inappropriate commentary. But achieving that expectation of a placid mood requires the utmost self-discipline from the teacher. Relentless patience is required. An almost supernatural capacity to anticipate both the predictable and the unpredictable must be cultivated. The teacher is then an artist of extraordinary power, a musician reading the score while improvising in consort with the entire orchestra. Stay on key. Don't skip a beat. Know when the piece has ended.

Among my friends and acquaintances, and especially among my former adult students, there are many who became teachers to rectify the chaotic cross-currents, the destructive hail storms and rending lightning strikes they suffered in childhood. In their childhoods the only constant was unpredictability. Even without violence, the sheer chaos of their early lives led to youthful escapes into alcohol, drugs, sex, and Internet addiction.

The familiarity of a predictable rhythm, like the columns on a Greek temple, can bear weight. Children crave regularity, structure, repetition, and form. The younger they are, the more the adult is called on to provide the day's architecture, to compose mealtime, to choreograph bed time. Predictable daily routines, recognizable weekly events, seasonal celebrations and festive anniversaries all contribute to profound security in a child. Maintaining a grip on time by marking its passage deliberately, instead of being yanked like a rudderless boat by conflicting currents and surges threatening to topple us, is getting harder and harder. Our personal devices and all their promise of saving our time are sinking us in their screaming demand for instant response. We, the adults, forget that time is not shackled to time-keeping apps. Time is elastic. Seasonal variations in the length of the days; daily changes in the shape of the moon; dawn, noon, and dusk as differing entities, these all remind us that time does not maintain a percussive beat. Rather, it breathes, and just as our own breathing adjusts itself and maintains us at differing rates, the way we maintain a sense of timeliness and order for children need not be absolute. Flexibility is fine as long as the basic pulse is maintained. When that basic pulse is maintained, the unexpected blip is far less upsetting, both to the child and to the adult.

Confusingly, children clamor for variations to the routine. And if we give in to their clamor too often, they get grumpy and become erratic.

How often have I heard the piteous entreaty, "Can we have class outside today?" It always sounds so appealing. Even in New York City, the 7th and 8th graders in particular would ask to go to nearby Central Park if they felt the conditions were favorable: teacher in good mood, weather cooperative. Then it took a lot of strength to stand firm, and to remember that every aberration to the predictable scheme of things would weaken the very rhythm that sustained us. That did not mean that we could never go out, it just meant that we didn't have to go out every time the children clamored beseechingly. There's a huge difference between giving in to a meaningless change of plans, and making a decision to change the plans.

As grown-ups, we know full well that the will to plow through all of the items on the endless To-Do List occasionally weakens. For some of us it doesn't so much weaken as ooze along, resisting our feeble attempts to squeeze ourselves into compliance. There's a reason for that old saying, "If you want something done, ask a busy person to do it." There are those who not only manage their lists without effort, but thrive on it. And amongst them, there are even a few who are not compulsively driven to empty their inboxes and check their To Do's. For most of us though, there is a hydra-like list: complete one task and two arise to take its place. The longer the list gets, the more listless we become. We procrastinate, we rationalize our procrastination, we psychoanalyze our rationalization, we flounder and flap and despair.

Just as diabetics crave sugar, the weak of will crave will-destroying activities, succumbing, eventually, to addiction, be it to substances or activities. A child habituated to rhythm, on the other hand, will more likely reach the choppy seas of middle age with a firm hand on the tiller, fortified by the placid childhood of sustainable seasons. As parents, we often indulge our need for adventure by traveling and holidays. The children, though, are sustained for life if they return to grandma's every summer, frequent the same beach, the same pool, the same camp ground year after year. It's a lucky child whose parents are ready to sacrifice their own desire for a change of scene, so that the child can benefit from the confidence inspired by familiarity.

Instead of promoting exceptional circumstances in the life of a child, it's up to the grown-up to keep them to a healthy minimum. Judgment is called for.

Where is that kind of judgment supposed to come from? Is there, perchance, a recognized scientific study that connects good judgment with a particular diet? And if there were, would we begin that diet? Or would we have the judgment to realize that it doesn't take a rocket scientist to realize that parental or pedagogical judgment relies on observation of the situation at hand. All the studies and surveys in the world are less about the child in front of us than what we can observe with our own eyes and ears, our own heart and soul.

What's gotten lost in our attempt to be the perfect parents and teachers, is just plain common sense, horse sense. What Scamp requires of me is dog sense, which consists largely of common sense, that in turn depends so much on good observation. Is the tail wagging? Tucked between the legs? Are the ears up? Hackles raised? Then perhaps it's a good idea to keep him close as we pass that other dog approaching us on the trail. Child sense is incomparably more complex. It requires the observation skills of an artist. We have to see the whole and the parts. We have to see the details, yet not be sidetracked by what we see. Above all, we must have the courage of our convictions, and once we are convinced of the importance of rhythm and predictable routine in the life of a child, we have to find the fortitude not to be distracted gratuitously.

Constantly changing your mind can seem to be a charmingly quirky mode in an adult. Its effect on children, however, especially very young children, even those who can't talk yet, is to rob them of true north. Just imagine that your local weather would become even more illogical than climate change has already made it, so that, for example, it could snow in July here in the Bay Area, where it almost never snows at all. Very young children are exquisitely tuned to their environments, and grown-up spontaneity is like the withering hoarfrost on a trumpet vine, except that black spots almost immediately will rise on the vine, whereas blight in a child can take decades to reveal itself.

Children are so tuned-in to adult needs, that they often compromise themselves out of loyalty and love. Commercial entertainment, which drives so much – the economy, the airwaves, culture, our schedules – was not invented by children. Nor, for thousands of years, was it necessary.

Enter any pet store and take a look at the toys for cats. There are swat and pounce toys, teaser toys, hunt-and-stalk toys, toys with catnip. There are plush cat toys and chewable cat toys. And there are blatant confessions. As one website devoted to all things cat states, "Having cats is kind of like having kids in the house - the parents have as much fun buying cat toys as the cats have receiving them."[26] And we haven't even started in on the dog toy industry, which, though huge, is just the tip of the iceberg in the toy industry world. As we all know, it is children who are the BIG business.

Tuli, my cat, has just jumped onto the table where a sewing machine is set up (a to-do item that has a self-sinking weight attached) and found a spool to keep herself entertained. There's also a cardboard box that can be knocked onto the floor. Tuli, it seems can entertain herself. Furthermore, that's just "entertainment" as humans see it. Playing with stuff, knocking it over. What Tuli is really after right now is my attention. Or more food. Or to be let outside, where what is entertaining is the front yard itself, and where Scamp is not permitted to be on his own.

As for Scamp, I used to think the right toy would prevent him from chewing on my furniture, but quite a few dollars later I can attest that it didn't. What he really needed was a risk-free environment. Now that he's an older dog, he no longer chews destructively. He simply outgrew the need as his teeth developed. Does he need entertainment? Sometimes he brings me a pull toy, or comes and leans his head on my lap. Like Tuli, he wants me to fuss over him and then, satisfied, he drifts off again.

Children have a way of checking in with their attending adults. What they want is to be sure the adult is aware of them. "Look, Dad, look, Mom, watch this!" If no adult is watching, the jump into the pool, the throw of the ball, the somersault all have less value. They are validated by an adult witness. If there is no pool, and no ball, a child will devise her own entertainment. Growing up in nature, for example, is a life-serving foundation. It fosters self-reliance and lifelong insights into the importance of small things, the importance of process. There are plenty of biographies to tell that tale. I am not advocating neglect. I am not encouraging loneliness. But I am suggesting that a child's appetite for self-created fun is swiftly corrupted by manufactured entertainment. This is true for children up through puberty. "Boredom" is a concept that has to be taught. No child ever died of boredom, but some primeval vein in our adult makeup, channeling guilt or fear or who knows what, buys into the idea that boredom is bad and, so indulged, the child soon forgets that a stick can serve to be car, boat, or jet.

We bring this concept of entertainment into our schools, and first graders, those wonderful inventors, sculptors, and engineers, relinquish their initiatives in favor of prepackaged coloring books and similar pablum.

Birthday parties with old-fashioned games can be a lot of fun. The very idea of "entertainment" at a child's party undermines what's being celebrated. Particularly in the middle years, 5th through 8th grade, the myth that ready-made trumps homemade easily takes hold. Yet it's just in these years that youngsters can appreciate the efforts of their peers, and enjoy the fun of making or solving a treasure hunt, to mention another old-fashioned favorite. Our children are spoiled by our adult need for variety, and our adult need for variety is buttressed and bewitched by the omnipotent fist of industry.

The simple life, in which choices are fewer, is now the privilege of the poor and the primitive. Soon, though, even the most local of cultures and the least privileged of societies will be tethered to megabytes. There is no going back to the simple life. We have to create it in our own homes, in our own classrooms. Uneventful days, rhythmically repetitive days, predictable routines, provide long-lasting, health-giving benefits, and we can but try to rescue time sped up by myths of our own making, in our cultural and personal lives.

Chapter Sixteen

Yes, but Do They Love Me?

Whenever I hear a teacher boast that, "The children are happy," I wonder what that means. 7th and 8th graders are happy at school when they are learning and working. They are disappointed and discontented when they come to school merely to tread water. Because it's not cool for a pubescent youngster to admit interest in school work, cool disdain for academic involvement is currency in the popularity bank. That's how "nerd" came to have its own identity. A nerd was a kid who was good at hard subjects, like math and physics. But those are the very subjects that lead to fame and fortune. So the word is confusing. Even its definition is bi-polar.

> nerd
> [nurd]
> noun, Slang
> 1.a stupid, irritating, ineffectual, or unattractive person
> 2. an intelligent but single-minded person obsessed with a nonsocial hobby or pursuit[27]

Whether stupid or intelligent, the nerds are having the last laugh in obsession-driven Silicon Valley, where they become part of the vaunted one percent by devising endless stratagems to lure teenagers into the false hope of Friends while isolating them in front of screens, be they handheld or full-size.

So successful do such nerds become that the word no longer has the negative connotation it once did. Students who do well at school don't have to be stupid, irritating, ineffectual, or unattractive; nor do they have to be intelligent and single-mindedly obsessed. The well-rounded scholar/athlete who works on the yearbook and volunteers to train seeing-eye dogs is still your prime college candidate but the teenage entrepreneur has popularized nerdiness and can count on fat college acceptance letters. Still, "the children are happy" is a slippery concept. What about the ones who don't thrive at school, or who don't want to let on that they like their lessons?

In preschool, the little ones are happiest when they are doing what is familiar and gives their imaginations free rein under the invisibly protective supervision of their teacher or care giver. By first grade, the child is having to conform to expectations. These can be met happily when they don't exceed the child's developmental capacities. Six- and seven-year-olds are happy in school when they begin to flex their learning muscles, which, as we've seen, requires a whole new set of behaviors, habits, and restraints. Although grown-ups are vainly ambitious for their children, no one would ask a six-year-old to snowboard down Everest. In many schools, however, the equivalent of skiing down a black diamond run is normal. Children are expected to take to the abstraction of written language as if they already had the muscles to do so. Some of them manage prematurely, and when as adults they are anxious and lack stamina, we wonder why. So the happy first grader is still in a mode of play, learning about letters and numbers through stories and pictures, painting and singing, gesture and verse.

Happy 1st graders think nothing of hugging their teacher. Happy 5th graders wouldn't be caught dead hugging their teacher. It's their engagement with the material, their absorption by the subject matter, their interest in their homework that shows their love and happiness. More and more aloof do the students become, and knowing whether they are happy and love their teacher requires ever greater discernment. In the many 8th grade writing courses I've taught, I've been astonished at the uncomplaining output of the students. I'm not an easy teacher. I don't encourage with false praise. But I do support every child's best efforts, by demanding something of them. You can't demand what is not there, but you need an open mind about what is possible for an individual child. Bad spelling, horrible handwriting, stormy punctuation, haphazard grammar – none of these interfere with my reading of a child's story. What interests me is whether the assignment, as it was given, was actually carried through. Did the child enter into the task? If that happened, and if it continues to happen, then we have the basis for beginning to work on the technicalities. Are the 8th graders happy? Only if I generate enough energy to urge them forward, ahead of me. Whereas in the lower grades the teacher is something of a gentle cowboy, herding the little dogeys forward and trying to prevent any from straying too far off course, the middle grades teacher is more of a cattle dog, nipping at their heels. The upper grades teacher is a scout, ahead of the herd, beckoning them into new terrain. At each stage, the children are "happy" when they are confident in their teacher. That confidence has to be earned.

The complete trust of a hapless infant or creature can be overwhelming. There's a lot of talk about the resilience of children. All of us survived childhood, so yes, we're resilient, because there is no such thing as a perfect childhood. But for the well-meaning parent, teacher or puppy owner, the responsibility is a constant challenge.

A dog is just a dog, as we've already noted. Scamp will never grow beyond his present level of consciousness. He's like a child of about two: self-absorbed, jealous, curious, alert when awake and adorable when asleep. There are things he likes, and things that scare him. He is playful. He has his own agenda. Unlike a two-year-old human, he is fickle and pragmatic. He will gladly follow any pied piper dangling an edible morsel. Unlike the toddling human, Scamp's limits are pretty well reached. It's not that I can't teach the old dog some new tricks, it's that the tricks will never develop into creativity, imagination, or utterances of soul.

Some decades ago, when I lived in Massachusetts, I had a dear friend whose big shaggy dog was not allowed into the house, even in the dead of winter. At the time I thought that was hard-hearted. I couldn't understand such callousness. Now I realize there was something really honest about it. The dog was not indulged. Neither were the children in the household, who grew up in an atmosphere of homemade fun, family culture, and nothing artificial apart from electricity. When your father is a sculptor, your mother a musician, and your home filled with beauty, you carry that atmosphere of steadiness and peace into your future. Those children are now in their 40s, with children of their own, and although I sometimes wondered how they would fare in the modern world, having been sheltered from it in childhood, they are successful in every way. They were never immoderately sheltered. They were just not prematurely thrown into activities they couldn't fathom. As for the family dog, he had a wonderful dog house, out on the porch. He would not have been influenced by the beauty in the house, though the regularity of life there, the rhythm of the days, would have served even him.

How can we be sure the child will love us if we don't indulge the child? Puppies and infants, in fact babies of every species, are designed to steal your heart. YouTube proves it. Babies of every stripe instinctively motivate their elders to feed, protect and groom them. Then the hapless, needy wee one outgrows that really cute and helpless stage. That's when we have to become more discerning to know whether they are thriving. Continual laughter is not a sign of happiness as much as it is a sign of hysteria. A frozen smile is a mask worn for survival, and might hide great misery.

It doesn't take much to keep Scamp happy. Nor do I need an almost mystical imagination to foresee his development. He will grow old and stiffen. He will not grow up to become a banker, pilot, oceanographer, or ski instructor. I can continue to keep him happy for years by providing him with the routine we've established. He loves me, and he'll love you too if you feed him and are nice to him.

Teachers and parents, on the other hand, face a new presence daily. Well, weekly. Okay, maybe monthly. Certainly and without question, yearly. Illness in a child is often a hiatus between the before and the after of change, a nodal point during which change happens. While the child is apart from the routine, he seems to slip into something new. Sometimes, after a child's illness, we can notice a change in the child's inner compass. There might be a new interest, a new self-confidence, a new strength. Day-to-day changes, interrupted by a mere night's sleep instead of weeks of illness, or months of healthy routine, are usually too subtle to notice.

Parents of newborns are sensitive to the slightest changes. Of compelling interest is their progeny's digestion. Enthusiastically, as if it were extraordinarily newsworthy, will they deliver a lecture on the content of the diapers. Every nuance of the baby's gestures is noted. By the time the infant has learned to stand, walk, and talk, even the doting parents can no longer keep up with the plethora of immense changes occurring from one day to the next. Suddenly the child can read. Suddenly the child can ride a bike. Suddenly the child has a driver's license.

I recently met someone I hadn't seen for over 30 years. At first, this stranger didn't strike a spark of recognition in me. After a while, though, the expression in the eyes, something in the visage, began to resonate. Three decades will weather most faces. Yet something essential remains, something of the soul and spirit. Where children are concerned, we tend to notice the physical changes, without paying enough attention to the inner changes. If we bring a degree of detachment to our observations of the growing child, we'll realize that the expression of the child's love changes as the child matures, and that it's up to us to recognize that love for what it is. Even when it doesn't look like what we think it should.

"See what I do, not what I say," would be the motto of most middle and high school students. We are surrounded by so much noise, cant, and hypocrisy, that it shouldn't surprise us when 6th graders pretend to be sophisticated, or 11th graders experiments with identity makeovers. The steadiness of our gaze can then be a tonic for them. Every rebellious pretense, whether lipstick in 5th grade, or tattoos, shaved heads, green hair, and sullen miens in 10th grade, is an opportunity for the adults to see beyond the obvious. What you see is what you get in a young child, especially in one not yet in a formal setting involving other children. No sooner is the child part of a group, whether in day care, preschool, or on the playground, then posturing sets in. Can we ignore the child's posturing, while confronting the child's behavior? That's where the teacher has the advantage over the parent. Uncompromised by the subjectivity inherent in a parent, privy to the child's accomplishments in school, the teacher ought to be able to provide the parent with an unparental perspective. Whereas a parent's happiness is so often dependent on the child's love, the teacher's effectiveness depends on relinquishing that yardstick. Compassion should not swamp the child. "Practice equanimity" is an injunction more easily followed by a teacher than by a parent. That should be an advantage both at school and at home.

When parents recognize that the teacher has a different task, and teachers feel free to take up that task without resorting to parental agendas, the child, from preschool through high school, is the beneficiary of successful teamwork. If all goes well, the child will find a steady center at home, and move in widening spirals through the world of school and successive teachers.

Chapter Seventeen

Taking the Show on the Road, Taking the Road to the Show

Travel is one of modern life's triumphs. I grew up as an airline brat, with a fistful of free airline tickets any time to any destination. The term "frequent flyer" hadn't been invented, but by the time I was eleven, I and my younger brother were featured in the Cape Argus (South Africa) Newspaper. The photo shows our dog, a shaggy Airedale, seated on a chair as we children lean over him to point at a small round globe in my hand. The caption reads:

> Eleven-year-old Dorit Winter and her brother, Amos (8), look at the globe in their Camps Bay home. Tomorrow they fly to Johannesburg on their way to Britain and then America.

Under the headline **Globe-hoppers pack again,** the text reads:

> To two Cape Town children – 11-year old Dorit Winter and her brother Amos, aged eight – travelling by air has as little novelty as boarding a bus. For when they reach New York soon at the end of their next air journey each will have flown more than twice round the world.

Evidently my father had kept track, because the article goes on to say that since my "flying debut" on my first birthday, I'd flown 47,692 miles.

The bit about "as little novelty as boarding a bus" was journalistic hyperbole. But flying was, indeed, familiar territory, so to speak.

My father was an airline executive, and until he retired in the 1970s, our family traveled the world *gratis*. The hidden price was the uncertainty of standby. I learned early that until the wheels had left the tarmac, we weren't guaranteed a seat on the plane. We once spent several unplanned days in Nairobi, having been offloaded during a fueling stop on the way from Zurich to Johannesburg. It was during the Mau-Mau uprisings; my brother got ill; my mother had no local currency; but what I mainly remember is the expedition to a nearby game preserve. There were hippos. There were giraffes. If memory serves, we arrived in Jo'burg on my 10th birthday, and my father, dapper as ever, stood at the foot of the stairway to greet us.

In those days, flying was, even for a jaded traveler like myself, a special event. You wore a nice outfit to the airport, changing into more comfortable clothes on board. Friends and relatives accompanied you to the gate, the pre-boarding mood was festive. As non-paying passengers, we were consigned to the empty seats, which often just happened to be in First Class. There you could even sleep in a fold out bed, or a hanging cubicle. Flight attendants were called stewardesses, and at take-off they offered you candy or chocolate or gum. All of which is to say that an aura of formality used to surround air travel before the deregulation of the airline industry.

Yet, even back then there were the unavoidable complications of delays, cancellations, and jetlag.

"Let sleeping dogs lie" is not meant to denote a canine's comfortable slumbers. Yet when Scamp is asleep, contentedness wafts about him. How much more palpable is the wonderful peacefulness hovering about a sleeping baby. It's no coincidence that, "Sleep in heavenly peace" is the refrain of that most iconic and universal of Christmas carols. A baby's sleep has something sacred about it. For grown-ups, sleep becomes profane, a necessity, not always successful. Having lost our connection to the other-worldliness of sleep, we think nothing of taking children on airplanes. Glibly we rationalize delays, cancellations, and jet lag, and the callous disruption to the child's space-time continuum. Not only is the circadian rhythm confused, the child's senses are assaulted. Ears, eyes, and nose have no way of shutting out the noise, fluorescence and odors of the airport and the airplane. Those sense impressions, for which sleep is the great processor, thus become stuck in the child's soul.

Scamp has two beds. One is centrally located in the living room, the other somewhat more remote, off in my study. My living room opens into the kitchen, and when I listen to the radio as I wash the dishes, Scamp wanders away toward the study. He doesn't appreciate the background chatter, even if it is National Public Radio. Nor does the mere clatter of dishes, without electronic commentary, need distancing. If the radio is off, or when live instead of canned conversation fills the living room, he opts to be part of the social scene. He stays.

Not until they count their birthdays in double digits are children impelled to create their own environments. That's when posters appear on bedroom walls, and personal desires in all sorts of areas – food, clothing, friends, entertainment – make themselves felt. So a speechless baby is a sitting duck. It cannot complain about the speed, let alone the noise, of modern travel. It must submit. And its one recourse, sleep, is compromised.

During a recent road trip with Scamp, I had the foresight to put his bed in the partitioned cargo area of my station wagon, something I'd never done before. He slept and slept, all the way down Highway 1, unimpressed during the frequent stops I made on his behalf, by the sunlit coastal cliffs. It was the first time I'd taken Scamp on an overnight trip. We were away for a week. Two of our hosts had dogs of their own, and I wasn't sure how it was going to work. But wherever we were, Scamp slept like the proverbial baby, in his familiar bed.

The proverbial baby has become a rarity. We interfere with their rhythms far too much. It's not convenient to honor their rhythms, so we wake the child willy-nilly, travel the world with our infants, and never think that those early experiences will translate into midlife symptoms.

Having started my headline making travelling career at age one, having racked up the miles to circumnavigate the globe twice by age 11, having continued to fly regularly and often up to and then beyond my father's retirement, I'm convinced that my vitality would be less compromised now, had I not flown so much as a child. Those would be interesting studies, correlating early travel in children with lassitude in midlife. Only, the variables would be infinite, and so such a study is unlikely. Jet-lagging a child clearly compromises a lot in the child's physiology; it's just that we haven't the discernment, or the willingness, to notice it.

Even travel by car has its cost. At-home births are still not the norm, and there's no getting home from the hospital or birthing center without a car. So most newborns are going to take their first trip when their age is reckoned in hours or days. Luckily, newborns are so enveloped in their own atmosphere that little of the outside world makes an impression on them. Their senses are not yet tuned and they manage to filter out most of the noise and flurry. Swaddling was the intuitive response to the newborn's vulnerability.

If travel is unavoidable, the obvious remedy is to get back to the routine as soon as humanly possible. If the routine can be sustained throughout the travel time, so much the better. For a child under three, parental determination can succeed in maintaining a routine but it will require sacrifice from the grown-up.

Just yesterday, as it happened, I chanced on this description of a syndrome I hadn't ever heard about, yet had intuited. Chapter Three of Dr. T. Berry Brazelton's autobiography, *Learning to Listen; A Life Caring for Children*[28], begins by noting

> In the early 1950s it was still assumed by many that newborn babies were 'lumps of clay' ready to be shaped by their environment.

It was one of half a dozen autobiographies I randomly picked up at the local library last week. He then goes on to cite a number of studies that show that newborns DO NOT respond to the environment. In his personal pediatric practice, however, he notices that they DO respond to their parents. His own observation of newborns and their parents flies in the face of the established academic medical research of his time. He decides to pursue his own research.

> If I could devise ways to evaluate newborn responses, I thought I could help predict the kinds of difficulties that an individual baby would present to parents.[29]

He finds a number of researchers, particularly child psychiatrists,[30] who have also noticed the anomaly between the clinical research and their actual in-life observations.

Well before all this research, parents already knew their newborns were responsive to light and sounds in the uterus. After birth, they could see the responses for themselves.

And then Brazelton gives us a sentence that every parent and every teacher really should take to heart.

However, most pediatricians, developmental psychologists, and neurologists hadn't accepted these observations.[31]

Here in a nutshell we have an authoritative statement about the difference between the authoritative experts and their theories, and the laymen and their practical experience. The theorists "were blinded to the full range of babies' responses by a flaw in the way they tested them[!]"[32]

Now we come to a description that ought to make the hair on your neck rise, such is the foolishness and stupidity of what is described:

To test sensory modalities in newborns, experts undressed them, laid them out on a table, and presented them with lights and sounds. The babies reacted only sporadically because they were protecting themselves from these intrusive sensations by "habituating," or **shutting out the sensations**. [emphasis added]

Here we have just about everything that's wrong with the testing model, as applied to test takers from newborns through high school – if not beyond. Conditions are created that make the test takers underperform and their capacities are cauterized for life. But back to the experts:

They [the newborns] might have shown reliable responses had the examiners brought them gently to a comfortable, alert state. As a result, no one would accept that newborns were really seeing or hearing. Parents' observations were not taken seriously.

Brazelton, who at the time was in his 30s then found a number of fellow travelers: A neonatal nurse in Boston, a neonatologist in Colorado, and a pediatrician at Yale. The latter …

… loved newborns and believed in babies' competence. She knew that you needed to support and contain them so they could respond. She would swaddle a newborn baby, wrapping his arms and legs with a blanket, then hold him in her arms at a thirty-degree angle, which alerts a baby. She'd sway gently in a rhythm to help the baby come to an alert state. As she virtually danced with the baby, the baby would become more alert. She'd sing quietly, dance slowly, and the newborn baby would open his eyes and become responsive to her. The newborn would follow her voice and her face. Sally demonstrated vividly that the baby could not only see and hear her but would respond when handled appropriately.[33]

In other words, here was a qualified expert who simply behaved like a mom, and lookit, the baby responded. It's pretty tempting to write "Duh!" in the margin.

Eventually Dr. Brazelton went on to develop the Neonatal Behavioral Assessment Scale, which is his legacy to pediatrics, and to legions of parents, and to all the babies who were not stripped naked and exposed to fluorescent lights and loud noises for the sake of science, were not, it would be accurate to say, tortured by well-meaning-ologists.

For our purposes, we've probably made the case. Even newborns, **especially** newborns, are all sense organ. They arrive on earth with built-in defenses: they can "habituate." In other words, they will stop responding to a stimulus after repeated presentations thereof. Interestingly, the term is used mostly in relation to nonassociative learning in animals, especially the more primitive species.

Of course, it's a way of life for most of us. Unless we live in the Garden of Eden, we endure unwanted sights and sounds as a matter of course. And come to think of it, even in the Garden of Eden, there were, as we all now recognize, unwanted sights and sounds.

The long and the short of all this is that habituation is a two-edged blade. It can enable to you to ignore the mind-numbing repetition of alerts through an airport intercom, or the irritating bark of a neighbor's dog (Scamp never annoys my neighbors!), but it can also numb your senses, your brain, your capacity to resonate with the universe.

I used to live in Sausalito, California, in a rented apartment with a killer view. Through a wall of floor-to-ceiling windows, you could enjoy the sweep of San Francisco Bay starting north of Angel Island and moving south past Alcatraz. This view was spectacular at every moment of every day no matter the weather. Even swirling fog provided a luminous light show. Alas! I became habituated to this ever-present glory, as I realized when first time visitors stood in my living room, captivated by awe and wonder.

So newborns, infants, children of all ages, and people in general live by habituation not under their control. It's necessary for survival and is most pressing in the youngest amongst us.

Yet, the thorns of life, as the great poet Shelley called them, force us to numb ourselves. Ironically, travel is one of the ways we seek to open ourselves to the world around us, yet, mindlessly, we thereby inflict overload on the sensory intake of children.

Instead of "habituation," which is an -ological term I first came across yesterday, I've been in the habit of using the term, "hardening off." Much in our culture contributes to the hardening off of children and adults. One of my favorite examples of this condition is the bare-armed, bare-legged northern Californian who is too tough to notice that it's cold enough to wear long pants and a jacket.

Having gotten this far in my ruminations, I continued reading Dr. Brazelton's book, and lo! He and I are in tandem – again! He too talks about hardening off. Because he is an -ologist and has a scientific, i.e. convincingly authoritative context, I would be remiss were I not to quote him some more. In the next section of his book, he describes how he developed the Neonatal Behavioral Assessment Scale, or NBAS. Leaning on prior work by a famous developmental neurologist, Heinz Prechtl, who had identified six states of consciousness in the newborn, Brazelton discovers that babies respond differently in each of the six conditions. He wrote of this discovery:

> It all began to fall in place for me. Unless one respected the state of the baby, you couldn't get reliable responses.[34]

Though it sounds simple, it is revolutionary. "Respect" for a baby!

Gerald Stechler [a colleague and child psychiatrist] and I demonstrated that newborns alert to interesting stimuli and put themselves into a sleep state in order to avoid repeated negative, intrusive auditory or visual stimuli.[35]

He now provides the details of how measurements were taken under scientific conditions to prove that newborn babies respond to external stimuli in predictable ways, and that the baby, after having "put himself to sleep to shut out disturbing stimuli," then awoke, "thrashed around, and by fussing and crying discharged the energy it had cost to suppress these responses."[36]

Now Brazelton comments on his own discovery:

This was an entirely new idea at the time – habituation followed by the discharge of energy to recover the **cost of suppressing responses to stimuli** that would otherwise overwhelm and disorganize the baby. [emphasis added.]

Here we have scientific proof that there is a price to pay for being overwhelmed. This is so germane to everything I've been trying to get at, that I will quote some more. It seems worth the risk of repetition:

As a result of understanding this ability to adapt, we came to realize that a baby's central nervous system was able to avoid overloading the cardio-respiratory systems by shutting out sensory stimulation that was too demanding. Habituation seemed to resemble sleep on the EEG. A baby who couldn't shut out responses to stimuli would be at the mercy of his environment. Normally, a baby has the ability to control his brain's reaction to a loud sound, a bright light, or repeated intrusive stimulus of any kind – visual, auditory, tactile or even kinesthetic. As he does so, one can observe his heart rate and breathing become regular and steady. As he moves into a state similar to deep sleep, he is "actively" shutting out all stimuli, and this costs him a good deal. But moving into deep sleep is not as costly as being responsive. He begins to breathe slowly and steadily, and his heart rate slows and becomes regular.

That is why, when neurologists or psychologists [Ologists!] in the past unwrapped babies (exposing them to cold air) and laid them out on a table (without any protection from their own startles), they would not see the babies' range of responses. These were noxious stimuli that the baby needed to shut out. At least half the time, babies would go into a habitual state. This meant that they often looked as if they could not "see" or "hear."

I then worked to figure out how to produce the baby's optimal performance. I saw that a dressed, swaddled baby acted very differently from an undressed, unprotected one.

For crying out loud! Naked and exposed, who wouldn't retreat. But no, we need a scientific study to prove it.

I found that babies lying down flat on their backs and at the mercy of startles that they couldn't control would not be very responsive. Held at a thirty degree angle [...] they would alert to a responsive state.

Okay. Brief interruption to note that "startles" is a noun, and "alert" is a verb. But let's continue:

As I played with newborns in the newborn nursery, I could get them to turn their heads, to follow my voice, my face, a red ball, or a soft rattle. And they'd work to stay under control, awake and responsive. When they became overwhelmed, they protected themselves with sleep, drowsiness, or crying. **I began to see these abilities as great strengths.** [emphasis added] They were critical to newborns, attempting to learn about the world – from the first.

And here, wonderfully reminding us that he is a mere mortal, and that he is writing an autobiography, he adds

As I found I was able to elicit these powerful abilities, I could hear my grandmother's voice: "Berry is so good with babies." [As a boy of 10 or 11 he used to look after 9 younger cousins, about which he comments 'I could keep them amused and safe and keep them from crying for up to two hours at a time. A miraculous feat, I realize today!'[37]]

Brazelton then delineates "A Newborn's Six States of Consciousness," before giving us several examples of how brilliantly babies communicate. These six states are worth knowing about because with just a bit of imagination you can see how they apply to older children as well.

> deep sleep
> light sleep
> an indeterminate state
> wide awake
> fussing
> crying

But back to the newborn:

As soon as I began to play with the babies using this concept [of the six states], it was like going under water for the first time with goggles and seeing all the fish one never saw before. [...] For example, when a newborn is crying in her crib and you lean down next to her ear and talk steadily to her, she will stop after a short bit and look up into your face gratefully. She has used your voice to help herself gain control. Or put a newborn up on your shoulder to cuddle her. Soon she will pick up her head, look around the room, mouth her fist, then nestle her soft little scalp into the corner of your neck. With a sleepy baby, hold her at a thirty-degree angle looking in your face, her own will alert as if she were ready to smile and vocalize at you. She wants you to talk to her softly in this alert state.

When you place a baby on the diaper table, holding her firmly, and talking while cleaning her, she'll look quietly and gratefully at you, ready to smile or vocalize. She will quickly learn that this is a time for communication. A newborn's responses are so thrilling. Whenever I'm with a newborn, I feel the magic in the way each baby plays a role in furthering the relationship with those who care for her, and, as a result, her future.[38]

A further part of this chapter deals with how parents can learn to understand their baby's body language. He again describes the need to "discharge energy" by crying or thrashing about.

Parents need to see how hard she [the baby] works to protect herself in deep sleep and how available she is to rouse from light sleep to an alert, responsive state. [...] In working with the NBAS, I saw how exciting it was to caregivers and parents to notice that as a baby follows the human face, she becomes even more actively engaged than she does with an object. Meanwhile, her motor activity and even her heart rate seem to be controlled so that she can pay attention. After a while, when she shuts off or changes to a fussy or crying state, the baby shows how much this interaction costs her immature nervous system. She is liable to be exhausted, to drop into a sleep state and become unavailable. It helps parents to know that a baby needs to recover before she can interact again. [...] A new parent begins to learn this language of self-protection. The baby seems to be saying, "I want to interact and learn about you and my new world – as long as I can." But when her system is overloaded, she seems to say, "I've had enough. Give me time."[39]

There we have it! Newborns, inarticulate and vulnerable, can take care of themselves. Overloaded, they retreat. It does not follow that the more articulate the child becomes, the less vulnerable it becomes. On the contrary, and that is what I was getting at earlier in this chapter, the more articulate the child becomes, the less it can protect itself. Language presupposes consciousness, and there seems to be an inverse relationship between consciousness and the innate capacity to process experience. Unprocessed, undigested sensory overload will lead to "a fussy or crying state" at any age. Enough! the soul screams, and we have a good cry, or fall into the cocooned chamber of depression, or the self-inflicted isolation of a breakdown or its less dramatic equivalent, addiction of one sort or another, including the compulsive need for the vicarious life of social networking or gaming.

The hermit in the wilderness, the monk in his cell, the ancient Buddhist in his cave, or the contemporary meditator on retreat, what are they doing if not filtering out the noise of ordinary life, minimizing the need to process external stimuli thus leaving the conscious mind free to set its own agenda? So overwhelmed is the conglomerate nervous system of our time, that even meditation has spawned an industry, and we are meant to swallow the ludicrous notion of "The Best Meditation iPhone & Android Apps of the Year"[40] without rolling our eyes or gagging.

The point is that ALL experience, not just the newborn's, requires digestion. But the older we are, the less passive we should be in the digestion process. Exposed and transparent to all that streams in, the child is totally dependent on the grown-ups to regulate its life so that an indigestible plethora of impressions won't result. Since the child will not be conscious of the problem until later, sometimes decades later, when there is a "discharge of energy," it is incumbent upon the grown-ups to be minders. That requires an enormous amount of courageous conviction, because it is not a notion that can appeal to a society fixated on MORE. Even when individually we, and especially our children, are aching for LESS.

"Faster, sloppier, more superficial," is the mantram-at-large. Educators are not exempt. Standards, measured by statistics and fed into software, dictate the rate at which facts are fed to children. No wonder the children get cynical. MORE say the testing measurements. LESS shout the children's hearts as their neurological and cardiovascular systems are over-stimulated. It takes real independence to avoid being sucked into this maw of standardized assessment in school, and minimize the keep-child-busy fervor after school.

The older the child, the more likely she is to buy into the self-serving premise of the adults. Then, when that child is in her 20s, she begins to see her early exposure to parental passions for what they were: a veneer, a carapace. Along the way, because it's just part of our culture, the child is hardened off and separated ever more from the "magic" of the protection of her earliest childhood.

Before leaving this topic, I want to consider another realm, which, like travel, is so romanticized in our culture, that to allude to its pitfalls is fraught with misunderstanding. It's the realm of competitive sports, and in this realm, unlike the realm of travel, I can't speak first-hand. I have, however, heard plenty of first-hand stories about its dangers. Googling "Danger of competitive Sports" yields 9,400,000 results. Here then is the 1st of 9,400,000 glosses on the topic.

Competitive sports for children expose malleable
bodies to repetitive actions, not only hardening them
into muscle bound mass, but not infrequently causing
life-long trauma. Professional athletes glorify the
tough physique. Working out is vaunted as the elixir
of life.

For most of us in the western, so-called "first" world, the
trajectory from the first car ride home after birth until
graduation from college includes massive subjection to
physical densification. A conglomerate of industries has
hoodwinked us into believing that muscle density is an
index of health. Here is another impossible subject for
scientific study: compare the quality of life enjoyed by
retired athletes, soldiers, dancers, acrobats, firemen, etc.
with those of older artists, poets, musicians, teachers,
philosophers, and other less physically stressed types.

I'm not advocating a life without exercise. I'm not even
advocating a life without sports. Personally, I loved netball
in my South African primary school days, basketball in
my high school days, tennis, which I taught at Camp
Glenbrook when I was 19, and skiing until I tore my
rotator cuff. I'm just trying to point out that children,
from an early age, are thrown into activities that don't
sustain their inner lives. Children love to move; they love
to play games; they love casual sports. They are defenseless
when the casual sports morph into parental or adult
ambition. Children will adopt their parents' values, and if
winning is all, and muscle mass is the yardstick, they'll do

what they can to adapt. They'll even soldier on into the world of, say, competitive gymnastics, and enjoy it for a while. Two of my former adult students reached national rankings in gymnastics. Injuries forced them out of competition around the age of 16 but they had already become disillusioned when they realized that they'd become blips in someone else's desires. Black belts and ballerinas, passionate, not to say compulsive, about their regimes, will be content to focus all their youthful zeal through the lens of their chosen recreation. But did they choose it? When they chose it, were they old enough to understand what they were choosing? Or did they emulate a sibling or relative, action figure or movie star?

Having an all-absorbing interest when you're in school is more important than ever. How much better to daydream about winning the match, the tournament, the championship, than getting lost in the haze of substance abuse. Yet when a physical regime becomes too intense, then the substance abused is the physical body itself. Too much travel too soon is a major contributor to the hardening off process, which encapsulates the growing human being in a carapace that suppresses the soul, albeit temporarily. Much later, in adulthood, if the armor is cracked – usually by life knocking us upside the head – we will do what we can to make amends by providing our own children with equal time for soul growth. It's all a matter of balance.

Providing children with opportunities for meditation will not balance a proclivity for hardening tendencies. Until they get to college, young people cannot yet center themselves through self-directed spiritual activity. They haven't yet enough of a Self.

It's always amazed me, again and again, that 8th graders are, generally speaking, incapable of judgment, incapable, in fact, of thinking. They can stridently take on a position, argue forcibly if not logically for it, but asked to evaluate a short story they really can't do more than tell you whether they like it or not. By 11th grade, students are beginning to think. And even 12th graders struggle to paraphrase Emerson. College professors are well aware of this deficit in their students, and the blame is often put on prior schooling. Even with the best of schooling, however, the capacity for thinking one's own thoughts, having one's own point of view, being able to analyze, or being able to come up with a solution that is not prefabricated, usually emerges as the youngster comes of age around 21. That's when spiritual practice begins to make sense, when one has a spiritual muscle to sustain it. Unfortunately for all the potentially innovative thinkers who are born, and by that I mean every baby ever born, because every baby is born with spiritual muscles, a muscle-bound childhood, a childhood with too much "habituation," clogs spiritual arteries.

Scamp loves to run. He is lean, all sinew and muscle. Given enough space, and the right conditions, which usually means just having a canine friend nearby, he goes into overdrive. I call that the "zoomies." He is really fast. Other dog owners frequently comment on his speed. Scamp won't get hardened off or become muscle-bound, not even if he joins the local fitness club. That's because he has no spiritual arteries. He knows, but he will never think. Scamp is self-reliant in many ways, but Emerson's "Self-Reliance" will forever elude him.

Not so the children. For as Emerson put it, "Nothing is at last sacred but the integrity of your own mind."[41] That integrity is worth preserving in the child, for it will allow her to remain comfortable in her skin instead of perforating her defenses with grown-up needs and ambitions.

Chapter Eighteen

Process

California's drought was recently interrupted by several days of blustery rain. Scamp does not like water, so to do his outdoor business, he crept through the pelting rain and back again as efficiently as he knew how. Would he were that efficient when I'm out in the park with him, poop bag at the ready. Our usual routine, a round of "Fetch!" in the morning and a brisk walk in the afternoon, was out of the question. Short-haired as he is, Scamp shivers when he's soaked. I went through several towels, rubbing him down after his forays, quick as they were, into the rainy yard. Dog people know that "boredom" is a worrisome aspect of a dog's life. Of course, boredom is a human concept, and even in children, boredom is usually a screen for some other missing element. In Scamp's case, without our twice daily hit of quality time, he made up for the deficit by finding other ways to attract my attention. He frequently came into my workroom to bat my elbow with his nose as I sat in front of the keyboard – an activity he finds exasperating. He often brought me his pull toy, in the hope that he could initiate some fun. Or, unable to get a rise out of me, he took to annoying Tuli, the cat. Having read Dr. Brazelton, I now know that Scamp is "discharging energy" when he gets fussy on rainy days. Animals, too, can be overwhelmed by too much sensory input.

Allow me to quote the developmental pediatrician just one more time:

> Your baby will tell you what works for her and what doesn't. Just follow her responses and behavior and you'll learn how to become a parent for her. You'll learn more from your mistakes than from your successes. When you try something and it doesn't work you'll try six or seven other ways to reach her. When one finally works, you'll have learned from all those seven or eight tries.[42]

Exactly. Observe. Observe. Observe the child. Observe the dog. They'll tell you what they need. The key, though, is that we can't give up the first time we fail to get the desired result. Note that he goes from "six or seven" to "seven or eight" without explanation or apology. Note that he doesn't say once, or twice, but half a dozen times and more. It takes the repetition of any practice for us to get good at observing, so that finally, after practicing our observations, we'll see what we need to see, and know what we need to do. Through continued practice of observation, we become our own experts. Observation, however, is not mere seeing. It's an objective, impartial, uninvolved, neutral way of seeing. Teachers have the better chance of succeeding. Their relationship to the child is professional, and thus, by definition, less personal. Still, even teachers have to practice such observation, repeatedly. So much of what we see passes us by without making much of an impression. Learning to see a child requires discipline and attention. Repeatedly. This repetition requires time. It is a process. There is no quick fix for process. Process requires time. Let's not talk about how time is being siphoned out of our lives by all our time-saving devices. We've already talked quite a bit about rhythm and repetition as the scaffold for growth. Instead, let's talk about how we can engage with process-in-time, and how we can integrate our growing children into a process as well.

Artistic engagement is consuming because it seduces the artist. Not for nothing are an author's books called his or her "babies." Personally, I don't buy it. But I do know that when an artistic process takes hold, it becomes a constant companion, a hum in the background. Everything begins to feed into the process. The book, the chapter, the page I'm working on, above all, the thought I'm pursuing, begins to tingle. Life's stray bits, like iron filings on a Chladni plate, manifest invisible force fields with designs we couldn't have thought up. Thus, I go to the library, mindlessly pick out some autobiographies, and lo, there is one that feeds directly into my current preoccupation. "Synchronicity" is how some describe this congruence of inner pursuit with outer banality. Whatever you call it, it bucks you up; makes you feel there is meaning, a hidden something that pops into palpable design once in a while. It gives you a charge, and you can go on.

Artists are so notoriously self-absorbed because they are so preoccupied. By that measurement, all children are artists, because they are so completely at one with what they are doing. So are gardeners, or ornithologists. You needn't be holding a pen or a paintbrush or a cello to rate as "artist." It's a matter of focus. So when the child is fussing, we need to be artists in observation, so that we can enter into a process whereby we inhabit the child's development. That was what Dr. Brazelton managed to do in spite of his medical training, his scientifically rigorous medical training that he excoriates in his autobiography.

It's a lot easier to watch the development of a painting, or the prose on your page, no matter how painful or painstaking, than it is to watch the vagaries of a child's evolution. Once we've grasped that a child is CONTINUALLY developing, we can begin to enter into the process by becoming conscious of it through observation, and then the process itself will reveal to us what it is we need to know. We need patience. It takes time. Instant everything notwithstanding, it still takes time for a child to develop.

And yet, even when we are patient, restrained, observant, and willing to take our time to do the research that observation is, we have to be ready for the unexpected flash of insight that can come our way. For each of us, in any profession, whether or not we call ourselves artists, whether we are engineers or brick layers or cooks, these are the moments that give us confidence that we're on the right track. We feel ourselves sovereign to the circumstances.

Scamp has a mind of his own, he can be contrary, run away when called, pounce on the cat, dig holes in the yard. But process is not a phenomenon he perceives. He tracks time with his stomach. He knows unerringly when it's dinnertime.

Speaking of which, it's time for Scamp to have some of my time. I'm going to go out to play with him. Sit! Fetch! Drop!

Chapter Nineteen

The Habit of Distraction, the Loss of Mindfulness, and the Impact on our Children

Regularity, repetition, and routine build habits in time and space, which organize the world for us and enable us to be in control. It is, as we saw in Chapter Two, a tricky balance because when habits calcify, they control us. Nevertheless, when a child's day is ruled by the dependable expectations of an orderly schedule, the benefits are far-ranging. Over time, benefits accrue if the growing human being experiences a continuously steady rhythm as activities diversify. One of those benefits is enhanced presence of mind.

Why is presence of mind, or mindfulness, the goal of just about any spiritual practice? Perhaps because it is so hard to achieve consistently. Meditation is the deliberate practice of undistracted mindfulness, usually for specified short periods of time. These sessions of concentrated effort yield results that, ideally, flow out into the rest of our day. Just as high-intensity exercise tones the body so that the body, which then remains toned all day, is ready to do what needs to be done, a meditative practice tones the mind so that the mind can then attend any circumstance with presence.

Presence of mind yields peace of mind. Engaged in the present moment, we're less likely to worry about the past or be worried by the future. Additionally, when we practice presence of mind, there's a very practical benefit: soul economy. With the mind at peace we not only worry less about what was or will be, we spill out less into the ups and downs of our feelings. We're more centered and more likely to regulate our passions rather than be regulated by them. While meditating, we find that our breathing becomes more measured; with presence of mind, we find that our interactions with outer circumstances become more measured. We become less focused on our self, and more focused on the circumstances at hand. It's not that our feelings are neutralized, but that we maintain equanimity in spite of our passions, that we don't get carried away by fear, anger, sympathy, or even love. With equanimity, which presence of mind fortifies, instead of being pummeled by the storms of feeling coursing through our souls, we can take note of them without becoming unmoored.

Though mindfulness can become a constant mode, that's an achievement few can boast. Most of us can be attentive for just so long. And by now it's a documented given that the ubiquity of technology – be it in our pockets, our hands, ears, bedrooms, bathrooms, cars, trains, planes, offices, hotels, resorts – damages attentiveness, undermines any striving to be attentive, and perforates our consciousness with distractions. It's no longer disputable. Attention science, attention studies, attention research have academic standing. A comprehensive overview of attention as subject for study is provided by

Matt Richtel in his work, *A Deadly Wandering: A Tale of Tragedy and Redemption in the Age of Attention*. Richtel meticulously describes how our own attention has, for some time now, sustained devastating neurological impact from technology, as well as our resistance to admitting it.

In *A Deadly Wandering*, Richtel exposes the fatal consequences of distraction through texting. Driving requires presence of mind; texting necessarily distracts the driver. His story is about death by texting. It's the ultimate in losing yourself to technological distraction. You can lose your own life and you can take the lives of others. In Richtel's story, the momentary distraction of a young driver kills two innocent people in a different car. Less dramatic than murder by texting, and a lot more prevalent, is the slow, steady, ongoing erosion of mindfulness that Richtel traces, and to which all of us are now exposed regardless of our intentions, just as all of us are now exposed to EMF – electromagnetic frequencies. Over time, our focus, like the geology of the Grand Canyon itself, gives way. Grooves are dug, the brain is refigured. Richtel has studied the terrain, and he was featured prominently in a series of articles in the *New York Times,* which wrote, "Articles in this series examine how a deluge of data can affect the way people think and behave."[43]

Think and behave!

In other words, these articles are about how our interactive habits affect our thinking and our behavior.

In his prologue, Richtel lays out the connection between technology and distraction:

> The onslaught [of information through technology] taxes our ability to attend, to pay attention, **arguably among the most important, powerful, and uniquely human of our gifts.**[44] (emphasis added.)

He goes on to discuss the genesis of attention science:

> Then, around World War II, modern attention science was born.[45]

> [Our gadgets] weren't just demanding attention but had become so compelling as to be addictive.
> The modern attention researchers...asked a new question: Was technology no longer the slave, but the master? Was it overtaking our powers of attention? [...] the concept that nips and cuts at attention in the cubicle can take a persistent and low-grade toll on productivity or in schools on focus, or at home on communication between lovers and parents and children.[46]

This newly spawned science has its own experts, one of whom is Dr. Gazzaley, who has become one of the foremost experts in the field of attention science.[47] This

Dr. Gazzaley, a colorful character whom Richtel presents at some length, recognizes that attention is "uniquely human." Dr. Gazzaley says that attention is also "absolutely critical for all high level functioning," a cornerstone of what it means to be human. He's not just saying that our attention allows us to survive – say, by being able to attend to a threat or perceive an opportunity. He means that attention allows us, in a "uniquely human" way to set goals and follow through on them without being distracted by every bit of stimulation around us.

This is essentially what Henry David Thoreau meant by, "Let us spend one day as deliberately as Nature, and not be thrown off the track by every nutshell and mosquito's wing that falls on the rails."[48] To avoid the distractions of nutshells and mosquitoes, Thoreau famously repaired to Walden Pond, where his self-determined life resulted in *Walden,* his master work, which became a pillar of American Literature. That was in 1845.

More recently, between 1986 and 2013, Christopher Knight hid out in the Maine woods, seeking solitude.

> "...the forest granted him freedom, privacy, and serenity. **And it transformed his brain** [emphasis added]. He developed photographic recall, a proclivity for deep contemplation, **a limitless attentions span**[49][emphasis added]."

There's nothing scientific about this conclusion; it's anecdotal. However, it perfectly corroborates the findings of attention science. Distraction, the overload of sense impressions, the too muchness of our 21st century lives, perforates our concentration and causes a sort of mindlessness. Twenty-seven years in the woods, on the other hand, led to "a limitless attention span."

It's a drastic solution to the overwhelm syndrome and neither feasible nor practical, effective though it was for Christopher Knight.

But back to the present with another quotation from Dr. Gazzaley:

> It [attention] allows us to interact with the world through our goals and not be led like a slave to our environment. It has allowed us to do every remarkable achievement – creation of society, culture, language. They are all dependent on being able to focus on our goals.[50]

Some 30 pages later, Richtel summarizes some of Dr. Gazzaley's research when he writes,

> In short, attention is extremely powerful and extremely limited.

He then ends this chapter with an unexpectedly apocalyptic conclusion from Dr. Gazzaley:

Distraction is a powerful weapon.[51]

Dr. Gazzaley, an attention expert, concludes that the undermining of attention through distraction is a weapon. Weapon against what? we might ask. The answer is obvious: against attention. Thus, by extension, against something "uniquely human."

What better way to attack what's uniquely human than to start with the young. Not only are children fair game, they're defenseless.

Technology companies are trying to get more of our brains per unit time. It's as close to a business model as you can imagine. The more engaged you are in what they create, the more successful they are.[52]

The sooner the child is "computerized," the happier the stock holders at Apple or Samsung. Holy smokes! Our children's brains are stoking the coffers of the attackers. Luckily, though, researchers and journalists like Matt Richtel and Todd Oppenheimer[53], and a cadre of concerned teachers, parents, and writers are fighting back.

The Science of Attention is no longer slouching defensively at the periphery. It's part of a growing backlash against distraction. The Science of Attention has legitimized the technological counter-culture, which champions what is uniquely human: individuality. In spite of the behemoth powers of the Emperors of Silicon Valley, the inner core with which every human being is born is, as yet, out of reach of the pandemic manipulations perfected by data management. Matt Richtel painstakingly proved what any open-eyed observer could see from the start, namely the tangled connections between technology, neurology, attention, and behavior. His detailed investigation, resulting in its conclusive evidence, vindicates the crescendo of alarms about the massive onslaught of technology. This vindication didn't come overnight.

Like climate change, a concept that also dripped into global consciousness for years before it overran the barriers of skepticism to become an evident danger, the attack on our consciousness by technologically-induced distractions is becoming an undeniable current.

Now that drought-parched forests burn, ice melts, and oceans rise, global warming is no longer a pathetic theory. Global warming has our attention. Climate Summits and Global Warming Conferences regularly grab the world's headlines. A decade ago, Al Gore and his "Inconvenient Truth" were scoffed. Now global warming is recognized not as an imminent, but as an existential threat.

Earth's only recourse is environmental damage and the hope that humans will recognize it while they can. Children have no recourse when it comes to technological contagion. Their elders, so often already infected, enthusiastically, and dare I say, self-servingly, disseminate devices whose sheen, now that they've been around a while, is dulling. And no wonder. Technology, as we've seen, has promoted itself shamelessly. So impenetrable was its early onslaught, that early criticism of its impact took courage. Among the first voices speaking up for the belittled "Luddites," a rebuke that took years to overcome, were the cautionary warnings of such writers as Sven Birkerts[54] and Cliff Stoll.[55] From their intelligent, thoughtful, and entirely ineffective criticism of technology's potential harm, to Richtel's Pulitzer Prize has been a slow uphill battle. There have been no Technology Warning Summits, no Technology Warning Conferences. But there has been a steady stream of clear-eyed publications.

Earlier on, in Chapter Eleven, we already met another of the early researchers to track the downside of technology, Sherry Turkle. At first she was an objective researcher, enthusiastic about computers, alert from the start to their power to dehumanize, but an observer nonetheless. In 1995 she published *Life on the Screen; Identity in the Age of the Internet*. Even by today's standards, Professor Turkle's credentials back then were impressive:

> The author is a Professor of the Sociology of Science at the Massachusetts Institute of Technology, and a licensed clinical psychologist holding a joint Ph.D. in Personal Psychology and Sociology from Harvard.

She is well-steeped. Her research is important enough to have warranted support from the Guggenheim, MacArthur, Rockefeller and National Science Foundations.

Turkle examined the social nature of an activity, which healthy common sense could have told us was intrinsically unsocial. She showed us that "our relationship to computers is changing our minds and our hearts." At the time, my own take on her efforts was that they were welcome and laudable but that her own mind and heart had, very understandably, been affected by her 20 years of involvement with the technology. Be that as it may, she evolved. In 1984 she published *The Second Self: Computers and the Human Spirit*. It was a transitional book in which she "defines the computer as more than just a tool, but part of our everyday personal and psychological lives."[56] The title was prescient. Over a quarter of a century ago, she foresaw that the Human Spirit was potentially at risk.

Then, in 2011, came *Alone Together; Why We Expect More from Technology and Less from Each Other*. By then, Turkle's perspective had shifted dramatically. She describes her daughter as the vital catalyst. Visiting the American Museum of Natural history with her fourteen-year-old daughter, Professor Turkle was brought up short when the teenager, after contemplating a giant tortoise from the Galápagos Islands, said matter-of-factly, "They could have used a robot."[57] What struck Sherry Turkle forcibly enough to pitch her into her next writing project, was that her daughter was "unmoved by the authenticity" of the turtle.

Alone Together is a thoroughly researched plea for authentic, direct, human communication. It's worth repeating the earlier quotation:

> Over-reliance on devices is harming our ability to have valuable face-to-face conversations, 'the most human thing we do,' by splitting our attention and diminishing our capacity for empathy. [58]

Here is a pithy summary of the very trajectory I'm attempting to track: our attention is split, our capacity for empathy diminished, and at least one significant element of what it means to be human, namely compassion, is being eroded. With this thought, a powerful relationship is revealed: the juggernaut of distraction diminishes our empathy, and thus blunts our morality.

Turkle's credentials, like her experiences, have grown. The book cover flap of *Alone Together* describes her as the "Abby Rockefeller Mauzé Professor of the Social Studies of Science and Technology at MIT, the founder and director of the MIT Initiative on Technology and Self, and a licensed clinical psychologist." To this I would add: Mother.

In children who are not yet plugged in, a virginal relationship to attention is still possible. Parents are often amazed by their children's patient preoccupation with Legos or doll houses, or feathers and sand. Just last week I was at the beach with Evelyn and her three year old son, Nathan. The toys his mom had packed for him were an old dented colander and two empty yogurt containers of different sizes. Soon the colander was sifting sand to be baked into a chocolate-vanilla-orange cake. Bits of driftwood became candles. Feathers added flourish. While Evelyn and I caught up with each other and the ocean boomed in the background, the child played contentedly, packing his baking containers, searching for "candles," checking in with us to ask what flavor cake we would like. The imaginary world a child disappears into is infinitely adjustable. When we grown-ups got restless and decided to stroll down to the water's edge, the child enthusiastically obliged, but he would have been just as happy creating another gritty culinary masterpiece.

The younger the child, the more complete is her identification with what surrounds her. She is all sense, which is why the textures, fabrics, colors, sounds, temperature, air . . . everything around her is so important. She breathes in her surroundings with less filtration than a tree enveloped by smog. Not only the physical atmosphere of air, water, and temperature, affect the child, but more rarified attributes of interest, warmth, love, and understanding become part of her inner life. Inner and outer are still united. Presence of mind and presence of body aren't separate. Nathan's joy as he watched the booming surf made him jump up and down in a jig of delight.

Having had his third birthday some months ago, this little boy had learned to navigate the world on his own two feet, had learned to give voice to his wants, is starting to grasp life's complexities. He is beginning to lose that total identification with the world around him. He's beginning to have thoughts that are abstract, unrelated to what he can see and touch. Nathan's incessant "Why?" was not really a question as much as a comment. When either of us adults took note of the waves, or the boats, or the surfers, Nathan's contribution to the conversation was invariably, "Why?" What he really meant was, "Wow, really?"

It is one of life's compelling ironies that in order to find himself and become self-contained, to become his own entity, a child has to withdraw from the myriad sense impressions the world makes on him. He has to lose the innate and intimate connection that, in later years, he might struggle to recreate. Then, to offset the world's too-muchness, he will try to return to that early state, to become one with the phenomena around him through yoga, or meditation, or art, or time spent in nature. As a child, though, he won't be overwhelmed, will keep his center, to the extent the world's impressions are checked, kept under control. Therein lies the constant challenge, to keep a balance between what the child can digest, and what the world throws at him. If the digestion doesn't keep pace with the impressions, concentration, of which every baby is a brilliant master, diminishes. At seventeen, the little girl who could once happily play with Legos for hours, requires a constant flow of interruptions, and Technology is happy to supply them: Snapchat, Twitter,

Instagram, Kik Messenger, ooVoo, WhatsApp, Instagram, Tumblr, Yik Yak – the list goes on and on and grows monstrously.[59] Hijacking attention, like the Yukon oilfields in danger of endless exploitation by greedy meddlers, is an activity so rife with pay dirt, that, in my vocabulary "Social Media Entrepreneur" denotes danger to the human environment no less than fracking.

What in English is called "presence of mind," in German is called "presence of spirit," *Geistesgegenwart.* That's the Genius of language telling us that when we are conscious of the moment, our spirit is present. That presence of spirit is what is sacrificed when the present moment is riddled with constant interruptions. The very thing that's "uniquely human" in us is strafed by the distractions that technology seductively lobs our way. All the authors mentioned earlier come to that conclusion in their own way.

Particularly drawn to the specifics of this seduction is Dr. Atchley, "an introspective former army captain turned scholar,"[60] and a psychologist at the University of Kansas. He is deeply, scientifically interested in why people knowingly indulge in potentially self-destructive behavior, like texting while driving. He asks, "Are these devices so attractive that, despite our best intentions, we cannot help ourselves?"[61]

In *A Deadly Wandering,* Richtel traces Atchley's research on the detrimental effects of technology on our consciousness. He points out that Dr. Atchley's question, "suggests that he's awoken from his own blind faith in technology."[62]

Dr. Atchley has clinically studied the dopamine surge we get from our cell phones, and he has conducted experiments to show that there really is a connection between the "lure of technology" and addiction.

> "That phone is literally a drug delivery device that rewards us multiple times for using it. It's no wonder people can't ignore it when it's in the car with them."[63]

The lure is so insistent that we become dependent on it. We become dependent on, habituated to, constant interruptions. The interruption gives us a hit of dopamine. We love it. We get addicted.

In fact, another of Richtel's subjects, Dr. David Greenfield, comes right out with this connection:

> "The pace of adoption of technology and cultural acceptance isn't that much different than the pace of adoption and cultural acceptance of the drug culture."[64]

There are "co-morbidities" that co-occur with Internet addiction: attention-deficit hyperactivity, mood swings, anxiety, and personality disorders. These lead to ...

… increased novelty seeking, low reward dependence, impulsivity, high risk taking, low self-esteem and disadvantageous decision making.[65]

The path from loss of attention to lack of judgment is becoming clear. The drum roll of Richtel's story gets louder, faster, and more inescapable. "To some researchers," he says, "it feels like neurological hijacking."[66] To which I would add that technological ingenuity is investing vast resources to exquisitely polish the lure so as to ensure maximum success at neurological kidnapping. Literally. It's no coincidence that the qualities leading to disadvantageous decision making noted above are rampant among our young. That most precious of human capacities, presence of mind, is under intense attack.

So there is now scientific data to confirm what every school teacher knows, that constant distractions undermine presence, whether presence of mind or presence of spirit. Distracted, we are not wholly present. A part of us is pre-occupied. Something in us is out the window, half asleep, lamed when we are not all there.

Illogical though it may seem, we can attend to the needs of others to the extent that we ourselves are "all there." Compassion, sympathy, empathy, these quintessential human modalities, require a strongly centered personality. Allow me to quote Sherry Turkle again:

Over-reliance on devices is harming our ability to have valuable face-to-face conversations, 'the most human thing we do,' by splitting our attention and diminishing our capacity for empathy.[67]

Our capacity for empathy! Let's consider some striking examples of "capacity for sympathy," yes, that would be compassion, as fought for and acquired in spite of oppressive, violent biographical circumstances by each of the following: Florence Nightingale, Mahatma Ghandi, Mother Teresa, Nelson Mandela, the 14th Dalai Lama, Malala Yousafzai. Here are individuals who overcame choking outer circumstances to achieve such luminous presence that entire nations took note. By being truly present in the face of overwhelming circumstances, their spiritual authority became palpable. Focus, concentration, discipline was the schooling they had in common.

Tenzin Gyatso, better known as the current Dalai Lama, personifies the instructive integration of centuries of learned traditions with great enthusiasm for contemporary achievements. It's a melding worth a closer look.

At the age of 24 he had to flee for his life.

The spiritual leader of Tibet, the Dalai Lama, has crossed the border into India after an epic 15-day journey on foot from the Tibetan capital, Lhasa, over the Himalayan mountains. Many thought he had been killed in the fierce Chinese crackdown that followed the Tibetan uprising earlier this month.

The Dalai Lama had to cross the 500-yard wide Brahmaputra river, and endure the harsh climate and extreme heights of the Himalayas, travelling at night to avoid the Chinese sentry guards.[68]

He fled a scene of chaos and carnage, and is, to this day, officially, a refugee. Nevertheless, his achievements are legion:

His Holiness has travelled to more than 67 countries spanning 6 continents. He has received over 150 awards, honorary doctorates, prizes, etc., in recognition of his message of peace, non-violence, inter-religious understanding, universal responsibility and compassion. He has also authored or co-authored more than 110 books.[69]

Here is a life of action determined by a "capacity for sympathy." He famously said,

Be kind whenever possible. It is always possible. There is no need for complicated philosophy ... the philosophy is kindness.

Clearly, his adherence to a philosophy of kindness is not merely an idea. It's an ideal he's lived. Yet, he is a man of the world. Does he have a cell phone? Probably. He loves gadgets.

As a child in Lhasa, Tibet, he taught himself to fix broken machines, from cars to clocks and movie projectors.[70]

His ongoing fascination with technology embedded in his authoritative mastery of Buddhism has resulted in the *Dalai Lama Center for Ethics and Transformative Values* at MIT. His education began when he was three; his studies were thorough and broad. Science, philosophy, and art were integrated. Consequently, spirituality and science are not polarities for the Dalai Lama and he can promote the fusion of inner and outer at MIT.

Personally, I'm convinced that it was the mindfulness toward conscious discipline, which led him to see the overlap of ethics and science. If he has a cell phone, he clearly isn't ruled by it. His incredible achievements attest to that.

Those are his worldly achievements, which don't yet make him a moral human being. Regardless of the moral achievements of Florence Nightingale, Mahatma Ghandi, Mother Teresa, Nelson Mandela, the 14th Dalai Lama, and Malala Yousafzai, their worldly claim to fame was predicated on their personal moral striving. In their striving they were so successful that they overcame the brute force of military might through their own personal conscientiousness. They were schooled to embrace a moral world order, and publicly at least, they were true to their moral compass. "Schooled" is the operative word here; mindfulness was a part of their schooling, part of their life's work.

Perhaps the easiest way to draw a line from mindfulness to morality is to point out that insanity is a legal defense. If you're out of your mind, you aren't expected to follow even the basic norms of society, let alone the moral niceties.

Part of the schooling of mindfulness predicates discipline, and discipline is so often a matter of deliberate habits. This brings us back to my contention that the habits with which we raise the child will ultimately influence the path that the human being takes toward, or away from, a striving for morality. Habits, as we saw in the earlier chapters, can be trained. The child cannot yet fend off the interruptions, the distractions, the endless attempts to corrupt attention, which an adult who has not yet succumbed to loss of focus, can still control. The child's claim to the individual inner life, which is his or her birthright, needs nurturing through the habits that can allow for maximization of all that is "truly human." These habits, and the child's inner sanctum require protection, especially from the rapacious attackers. Technology as childcare is detrimental, right into the brain's physiology. Baby apps destroy mindfulness, undermine centeredness, weaken the moral compass. The global escalation of amoral and immoral actions is so devastating, that the individual can seem merely to cling to desiccated roots where once whole forests flourished.

It is my contention that by supporting every child's birthright of involvement through the appropriately escalating expectations of habits of thought and habits of behavior, we re-enliven the planet. This is why the mindful education of the child is paramount.

As we've seen, Scamp is mindful only of his stomach, his nose, and his master, me.

He's nudging my elbow. I wonder what he wants.

Acknowledgements

Michael and Yelena Tcheng confidently allowed me to use their own, and their children's, real names. Carol Williams read the very early versions of the manuscript and provided honest, helpful feedback. Diane David read the manuscript in-process and made valuable, encouraging suggestions. Naomi Kalfa kindly took on copy editing. Chantal Valentine generously offered her children, time and camera for help with pre-publication publicity. Afshin Jalalian cheerfully provided hours of photographic expertise. Margrit Häberlin developed the art of touch screen line drawings, and helped solve the mystery of the cover. Sean Chiki unhesitatingly agreed to lend his professional skill and his illustration provides the end piece. Mia Terziev and Kate Kristensen ably corrected the proofs. Jo Anne Smith (intuitiveleaps.com) deftly designed the book and tactfully offered professional guidance. Sincere thanks to each of them. Whatever mistakes remain are mine entirely.

To all who supported me in various ways while I was working on this book, you made a real difference, and I appreciate it beyond measure.

To all who contributed to the "Red Wheelbarrow Fund," profound gratitude.

About the Author

Dorit Winter, MA, brings a cosmopolitan background to all her undertakings. Born in Jerusalem, she attended kindergarten in Zürich, primary school in Johannesburg and Cape Town, and junior and senior high schools in New York City.

During her long career as a teacher, she taught a variety of subjects in grades 5-12. As an adult educator, she focused mainly on teacher training.

Dorit retired in 2014 and continues to be active as an author, tutor and teacher, mentor and advisor, and speaker and workshop leader. She lives with her dog, Scamp, and cat, Tuli, in the San Francisco Bay Area.

Please send corrections, reviews, commentaries and responses, as well as requests for author events such as book signings, workshops, presentations and consultations to dandelionpublications.info@gmail.com.

Endnotes

[1] http://www.dictionary.com

[2] http://animals.howstuffworks.com/animal-facts/dog-show1.htm

[3] What about the abnormal child? This would constitute an entire book in itself. Briefly, my take is that every child is "normal" but some children have infirmities that interfere with their development. These are the "children in need of special care" and their caregivers have challenges, which I am not addressing here.

[4] Waldorf pre-schools excel at this sort of thing.

[5] Dictionary.com. The American Heritage® Dictionary of Idioms by Christine Ammer. Houghton Mifflin Company. http://dictionary.reference.com/browse/tight ship

[6] *To Sir With Love,* by E.R. Braithwaite; Bodley Head, London, 1959.

[7] http://www.sandiegoreader.com/news/2001/nov/15/dogs-can-smell-better-people-exactly-how-much-bett/#

[8] http://www.pbs.org/wgbh/nova/nature/dogs-sense-of-smell.html

[9] http://www.answers.com/Q/How_much_better_can_a_dog_smell_than_a_human

[10] ibid

[11] ibid

[12] http://dogs.petbreeds.com/l/45/Cavalier-King-Charles-Spaniel

[13] http://www.theatlantic.com/technology/archive/2015/10/reclaiming-conversation-sherry-turkle/409273/

[14] Family Man by Calvin Trillin, Farrar, Straus and Giroux, New York, 1998.

[15] ibid. p. 5

[16] http://www.npr.org/2014/07/11/330692780/in-a-remarkable-feat-boyhood-makes-time-visible

[17] *Family Man* by Calvin Trillin, Farrar, Straus and Giroux, New York, 1998, p. 158.

[18] "The female Bildungsroman (or novel of development) is, in some ways, a contradiction in terms." See: http://the-toast.net/2016/02/18/eight-classic-female-bildungsromane/

[19] http://www.princeton.edu/~achaney/tmve/wiki100k/docs/Bildungsroman.html

[20] http://education-portal.com/academy/lesson/bildungsroman-definition-characteristics-examples.html#lesson

[21] http://www.goodreads.com/shelf/show/bildungsroman

[22] 516 titles came up on https://www.goodreads.com/shelf/show/dog-stories

[23] It would be a sin of omission if I did not at this point mention the debut of the new NPR show, Invisibilia, "a show about invisible forces that control human behavior." Their show, Locked-In Man, has caused a buzz. My read is that the buzz comes from our human powers of compassion, which helpless suffering, especially at the hands of well-meaning but unperceptive people, causes.

[24] https://en.wikipedia.org/wiki/Food_industry

[25] http://www.wired.com/2015/01/nyc-blizzard-subway-shutdown/

[26] http://cats.about.com/od/playforcats/tp/cat_toys.htm

[27] *The Dictionary of American Slang.* From Dictionary.com website: http://dictionary.reference.com/browse/nerd

[28] Learning to Listen; A Life Caring for Children, by T. Berry Brazleton, MD, Da Capo Press, Boston, 2013.

[29] ibid, p. 45

[30] See especially Stella Chase and Alexander Thomas

[31] Brazleton, p. 47

[32] ibid p. 48

[33] ibid. p. 49 ff

[34] ibid p. 51

[35] ibid

[36] ibid. p. 52

[37] ibid p. 6

[38] ibid p. 55

[39] ibid p. 58 ff

[40]http://www.healthline.com/health-slideshow/top-meditation-iphone-android-apps

[41]Ralph Waldo Emerson, "Self-Reliance."

[42]ibid p. 58 ff

[43]http://topics.nytimes.com/top/features/timestopics/series/your_brain_on_computers/index.html

[44]A Deadly Wandering, Matt Richtel, William Morrow, New York, NY, 2014, p. 4

[45]ibid

[46]ibid p. 5

[47]ibid p. 32

[48]*Walden*, Henry David Thoreau, Chapter 2

[49]"Lessons of the Hermit" by Nathaniel Rich, in the *Atlantic Monthly*, 2017. Book review of *The Stranger in the Woods: The Extraordinary Story of the Last Hermit*, by Michael Finkel. Knopf. March, 2017

[50]ibid p. 35,

[51]ibid p. 71

[52]ibid p. 109

[53]The Flickering Mind: Saving Education from the False Promise of Technology; Penguin Random House, 2003

[54]The Gutenberg Elegies; The Fate of Reading in an Electronic Age, Sven Birkerts; Fawcett Columbine, New York, 1994

[55]Silicon Snake Oil; Second Thoughts on the Information Highway, Knopf Doubleday Publishing Group, New York, 1996. High Tech Heretic; Why Computers Don't Belong in the Classroom and Other Reflections by a Computer Contrarian, Clifford Stoll, Doubleday, New York, New York, 1999.

[56]https://mitpress.mit.edu/books/second-self

[57]*Alone Together; Why We Expect More from Technology and Less from Each Other,* Sherry Turkle, Basic Books, New York, 2011, p. 3

[58]http://www.theatlantic.com/technology/archive/2015/10/reclaiming-conversation-sherry-turkle/409273/

---

[59]https://www.commonsensemedia.org/blog/16-apps-and-websites-kids-are-heading-to-after-facebook. NB: each app is described and followed by a "What parents need to know" list. Compiled 3/1/16.

[60]ibid, p. 139.

[61]Richtel, p. 141

[62]ibid

[63]http://www.zoominfo.com/p/Paul-Atchley/88144051

[64]Richtel, p. 193

[65]Richtel, p. 197 ff

[66]Richtel. p. 215

[67]http://www.theatlantic.com/technology/archive/2015/10/reclaiming-conversation-sherry-turkle/409273/

[68]http://news.bbc.co.uk/onthisday/hi/dates/stories/march/31/newsid_2788000/2788343.stm

[69]http://www.dalailama.com/biography/a-brief-biography

[70]http://thecenter.mit.edu/cent_press_room/dalai-lama-center-to-open-at-mit/

Made in the USA
San Bernardino, CA
01 September 2017